The Relentless Pursuit
of Greatness

Thomas R. Williams

with Kathleen Birmingham

THOMAS R. WILLIAMS, INC.
LOS ANGELES, CALIFORNIA

D1089506

Thomas R. Williams/Thomas R. Williams, Inc.
578 Washington Boulevard, #428
Marina del Rey, CA 90292
www.ThomasRWilliams.com

Book Layout ©2013 BookDesignTemplates.com
Photos: Scott Tokar Photography
Cover Design: Matt Coyle

For Quantity Sales, Ordering Information, Speaking Engagement Information:
Please go to www.ThomasRWilliams.com/contacts.html

The Relentless Pursuit of Greatness/ Thomas R. Williams. —1st ed.
ISBN 978-0-9905374-2-7

Contents

PART I - IDENTITY

Student - Athlete.. 3

Before It Gets Easier 9

Sick and Tired . . . of Being Sick and Tired 17

PART II - BECOMING A MAN

Asking For Help.. 29

Adversity – Academic Obstacles and the Injury Bug 39

Time Management 49

Showing Up.. 57

Taking Charge of Finances 63

Ownership 77

Social Media – What is Your Brand? 85

PART III - LEGACY

Giving Back 97

Networking – Part I.. 109

Networking – Part II... 117

Relationships 129

Leadership 141

PART IV - TRANSFERRABLE

Transferrable Skills 151

Mentorship 161

Internships 173

Resume 185

Exit Strategy 195

Still Playing the Game 207

PRAISE FOR
THE RELENTLESS PURSUIT OF GREATNESS

Failing to plan is planning to fail. Bill Belichick taught me that the answers to the test I would take on Sunday's on an NFL field were all on the tape. The only question was, would I watch the tape? Thomas is giving you the answers to life's test waiting around the corner. The only question is, will you listen?

~Heath Evans- NFL Analyst, Former NFL Player

Thomas' candor about the variety of challenges he faced on his journey will certainly resonate with other elite athletes. His book is more than a memoir in that it forces readers to reflect on their personal experiences while also providing a blueprint for how to prepare for their life after sport. Currently, the majority of elite athletes do not spend enough time on personal development, which makes their transition to a non-sport focused life more difficult. All elite athletes should benefit from this book's effort to act as a guide for them during this transition and allow them to prepare better for what lies ahead.

~ Jon Harris, Founder/CEO AthLife & The AthLife Foundation

The relentless pursuit of greatness is an essential read for any athlete about to embark on their collegiate career. It provides a necessary life skills education that so many in college have to learn the hard way. Basically ,this book is the instruction manual for success in collegiate athletics.

Josh Lifrak, MLB Mental Skills Director

I am so impressed by Thomas and his ability to transcend the plank of transition into a world where sports is no longer an identity. He is the most invaluable resource to student athletes, and there is no better real-life example. We are all inextricably linked to our sport, but that also paves the bond we can build as teammates in our new chapters, whether it be networking, community, or any other pursuit of greatness.

~Justin Blaine, Co-Founder Athletes Touch

Dedication

Dad, over the years, I have watched you go through so many transitions. In honor to you and to my readers, I dedicate this book to you.

You helped me in many ways during my college and NFL career; the phone conversations, the text messages, and the constant reminder that "The race isn't given to the swift, or the strong, but the one who endures to the end." You made many cross-country trips to watch me play, even though we could only spend a few short moments together after the game. Through it all, you listened to my fears, uncertainties, and insecurities, all without judgment.

I am most thankful to you for your words the night I was forced to leave the game forever: "Thomas, your words will be more impactful than any hit you had on the football field." I have never forgotten those words and they have created the path for my feet ever since.

Thank you, Dad.

Love, Thomas

Foreword

I wrote this book for one simple reason.

I want to help the reader discover their answers for some of the hardest life questions we have to answer. Life is all about transition, and I designed this workbook to get every single student athlete to answer the "what's next?" question.

I hope by reading this book, you are inspired to look beyond my experience and look into your own lives for the answers that resonate with you. There are no right or wrong answers in that you'll be graded at the end of the book. What is right or wrong depends entirely on you.

Answering the questions after each chapter gives you the courage to look around the corner. What *is* after your college athletic experience?

If you don't know, you've picked up the right book.

Acknowledgments

I thank Mom and Bob for never missing a home game. The memories and experiences from those five years will always be an amazing time in our lives.

Pete Carroll, Coach, thank you for recruiting a small town kid to come to a big city. You not only taught me how to win on the field but more importantly how to compete so I could win forever!

Ken Norton Jr., Coach, you are one of the biggest reasons I am the man I am today. Thank you for teaching me how to defeat a block and how to take on life. See you at the top!

David B. Scott, a.k.a. "Pops," thank you for seeing more in me than I could see in myself. You never let me see myself as *just* an athlete, and I will forever appreciate you for it.

Scott and Kelly, meeting you both may have been by accident but I am forever grateful for our purpose. Thank you for your everlasting love!

Kathleen Birmingham, thank you for always helping me tell the "perfect story." You have helped me change so many lives.

Keith Rivers, thanks for always challenging me to think beyond the norms. I am grateful for our experiences on the field and look forward to the memories we create for the rest of our lives. Fight ON!

Jeff Byers, your knowledge and wisdom shared in this book will not only open the eyes for all student athletes but you have also given them applicable tools to help change the trajectory of their lives.

There are many of you, too numerous to list here, who gave me encouragement, advice, listened to my dreams, and nightmares. You all know who you are, and you know how special you are to me. I want you to know I appreciate you for having been with me along this journey.

Let it be known, I appreciate everyone who has helped me along this journey.

Introduction

Dear Reader,

As 18-year-old freshmen transitioning into college, our main focus is to get to class on time, learn as much as our brains can retain, work out, go to meetings, practice to the point of total exhaustion, perform to the best of our abilities on game day, and then graduate.

The two main goals for most of us are to graduate with a degree on the way to, hopefully, going pro in our sport.

We have all heard how small the percentage of athletes who continue their careers after college. The truth is, as athletes, we *all* have an expiration date, whether it is our last game in college or our last game professionally, we *all* have to retire.

100% of us.

When I knew my NFL career was over, I found myself wishing for a playbook to guide me through this next transition.

I realized there wasn't one.

Throughout our athletic careers, we get playbooks to show us how to be successful in our sport. We get weight room routines to become better athletes. We get books and syllabus for each class to show us the best route for success in our studies. What about navigating the journey to the next phase of our lives?

Where is *that* playbook?

I've talked with many people who face transition in their lives, most of them athletes.

The biggest fear they express is they're worried about their future.

They ask, "Is this all I am?"

They don't know who they are.

That's where this book, this **playbook,** starts. Part I deals with identity, those who find themselves starting all over again, asking, "Who am I?"

If you don't know who you are, you might try to be something you are not, which leads to negative feelings. Many former professional athletes admit they still identify themselves as athletes, even though their careers are over. They don't know how to proceed. They don't have the playbook that helps them answer the question, "What's next?"

I wrote this book to help you understand you are great.

Yes!

Already, you are a great athlete.

As great athletes, you have incredible abilities with transferrable skills that will serve you well whether on the field or that next play you plan to run for the rest of your lives.

You never have to stop being successful in life.

The jersey may collect dust and you may never do another wind sprint after you stop playing, but your individual greatness is something *only* you can pursue.

You are more than an athlete.

More than a number on a jersey.

More than the points you score.

If you use this playbook well, you will see getting an education is equally important to winning the next National Championship.

The time you spend in college is when you invest in your future.

Muhammad Ali said it best, "Work hard now, and live the rest of your life as a champion." I think that is also true when it comes to student athletes in college.

Each chapter in this book deals with an essential issue or skill student athletes must focus on in order to invest well in their future. I ask questions at the end of every chapter to help you discover who you are and what your future could look like.

There is no time to waste because the future is right around the corner.

This playbook will help you to maximize your time in school, teaching you to be more than an athlete.

You're surrounded by people who want to know you; invest time in that. Find out who you are when you're not competing as an athlete.

Explore and discover what you like to do outside of playing sports.

That way you won't wind up doing something you hate for the rest of your life.

I hate to say this. The reason most of us have such a hard time moving on in life after sports is because we did not fully understand the game would end.

We thought the game would continue forever.

It doesn't matter if you go on to play professionally for a decade after college and make all of the money in the world. You will still have to answer the question, "What's next?"

The day you stop playing your sport is the day you become a "former" athlete. Prepare for it at the same time you're continuing to be great at your sport. That way, when the question of "what's next?" comes up, you'll have an answer.

The Relentless Pursuit of Greatness is your playbook for while you're a student athlete and afterward. Use it wisely to get an education, make some memories and put yourself in a position to be ready for the rest of your life.

The Relentless Pursuit of Greatness has nothing to do with playing sports. Instead, it is a lifestyle, giving you permission to keep living long after your playing career.

I want every single student athlete to know you have the opportunity of a lifetime while playing sports for your university. All of us as athletes can only run so fast, jump so high, and get so strong.

There is a limit to our athletic abilities.

As for our lives, we can become as great as we want to be. The choice is legitimately up to us, no matter how your athletic career pans out, there is another game to be played.

That game is life.

You never have to stop playing the game.

The same skill sets that made you an athletic phenom are what will allow you to experience the same success in the everlasting game of life.

Look over this playbook.

Study it. Memorize it.

Allow it to change your life.

Sincerely,

Thomas R. Williams

PART I

IDENTITY

CHAPTER 1

Student - Athlete

Who Am I?

When I headed off to college, I thought I had a pretty good idea who I was as a person. I'd been raised to be polite, respectful, and obedient. As we all do, I observed the behavior of other people, watching to see if their actions were effective in getting them what they wanted out of life. When I reached USC, I came from a sleepy small town in northern California and traveled to one of the biggest cities in the country. There, my field of observation expanded and I began to notice more varied behaviors, some of which I'd never considered using.

Before I got to USC, I figured I was just me. Once I realized we all have alter egos, I could look back and see how I used different parts of myself to show up in different areas of my life.

Developing an Alter Ego

For example, when I got to college I was the same kid on the field as I was off the field.

I was more focused, and certainly more aggressive when playing football, but I still was the same polite, respectful, and obedient Thomas Williams I was outside the lines.

There was no light switch.

But that wasn't working for me. After a game against the Cal Bears, I ran past Coach Carroll and he said, "Here comes the Hitman." It made me feel I had an athletic identity.

Initially, it was very difficult for me to embrace that.

Was I Thomas or The Hitman?

Who, exactly, *was* the Hitman? How could I call on him when I needed him? Even more important, how could I turn him on and then off? This might even sound a little like multiple personalities to you, but it isn't. There are times in our lives we need to be soft, compassionate, and gentle. There are times when we need to flip the switch, and dig deep inside ourselves so we can tap into our individual greatness. The key is when you are in a particular setting, *that* is who you need to be there in order to maximize your full ability. When you are in another setting you must be *that different* personality in order to get the best results. When you understand *who* you are, *where* you are, you can then maximize what you're doing.

I finally discovered I could not be the Hitman in the classroom and I couldn't be Thomas Williams while I was on the football field. If I tried to be the Hitman in the classroom, I would not be the best student. In fact, I'd probably be a reactive, disruptive student, just as I desired to be on the football field.

In the same vein, I couldn't be Thomas, the student, on the football field. Can you imagine saying, "Excuse me, do you mind if squeeze by you so I can sack your quarterback?"

Ridiculous! Right?

So how do you identify this alter ego, and how do you bring it out?

The Hitman

After Coach Carroll called me "The Hitman," I was really excited. I had an athletic identity. I could really *be* someone completely different on the football field. I had a problem. I didn't know how to turn him on.

I had to figure out how to turn the Hitman on and off. For me, it was a matter of watching film of some of my football heroes. One in particular was John Randle, a defensive lineman for the Minnesota Vikings. He was a crazy man on the field! He painted his eyes black; he looked a lot like a raccoon. He talked all game long, shouted things to keep himself and his teammates pumped up the entire game. Watch a video of this guy and you'll see the true meaning of an alter ego.

I used him as a role model. I started painting black streaks on my face. At first, even some of my teammates made fun of me. When I put that black war paint on, I armed myself for the upcoming game. Mentally I was preparing myself to become a warrior; a crazy, high-energy, dynamo while I was in uniform. Just as clowns and certain actors stay in character when they are dressed in costume, when my face was painted and my uniform was on, you were no longer seeing Thomas.

I became the Hitman.

Not everyone needs a physical cue to make that type of transition, but for me it worked more effectively than anything else I'd ever done. Some people talk about wearing a pair of lucky socks, or a certain shirt or tie before going in to a very important meeting. Whatever *you* need to do, do it. If you can learn how to adopt this alter-ego persona, you're way ahead of the competition. When you have an alter ego, identify it, embrace it.

When you embrace it, you become it.

Just Plain Thomas

Once the game was over, the pads came off. I washed my face and became me again.

Just plain Thomas.

I'm quiet, respectful, easy to talk to, and not at all aggressive, loud, or obnoxious. For some people, this was a very strange transition. I enjoyed it every time a person would ask, "How can you be so aggressive and energetic on the field and the complete opposite off the field?" I took it as a compliment. That means I'm assuming the role of my "alter ego" correctly. I use it when I need it, and I can turn it off when I don't. This little trick is one of the biggest secrets of successful people throughout the world. Take it. Add it to your bag of tricks and know your greatness lies in your alter egos.

There is no limitation on greatness.

Greatness is your own capacity to be the very best you were created to be.

Questions:

Think about who you are as a student: List 2 characteristics you want to be known for as a student:

1.

_____

_____

2.

_____

_____

Think about who you are as an athlete: List 2 characteristics you want to be known for as an athlete:

1.

_____

_____

2.

_____

_____

What is the best way you know how to transition into student mode?

_____

_____

_____

_____

How do you flip the switch to become the competitive athlete?

_____

_____

_____

_____

You are both a student AND an athlete! When you can identify who you want to be in each setting, that is when you give yourself the best opportunity to maximize your greatest abilities.

CHAPTER 2

Before It Gets Easier . . .

It Won't Get Easier, You Just Get Better

When I left Vacaville for USC after high school graduation, I kept telling myself I made it! My lifelong dream had come true. All those sprints, pushups, and extra reps in the weight room had given me a one-way ticket out of Hamburger Hill. This is the name given to a part of Vacaville where a bunch of hamburger joints were clustered, and I remember one night Mom drove us by that area and all I could think was, "I gotta get a scholarship. It's the only way out of Hamburger Hill."

As the plane made a soft landing, the captain came over the intercom and said, "Welcome to L.A." That sounded pretty good, home of the movie stars and celebrities. I walked through the airport looking for the baggage claim signs when I suddenly came to the realization I was alone. No one was there to make sure I had everything together. No coach was there to usher me as they had done for my recruiting visit. It was all up to me. I couldn't help but smile and walk with a little bit of a swagger. I had finally reached LA as a USC football player. This was all I ever wanted. I wanted to tell every person in the airport who I was and what I was doing there. This was how I always wanted it to be.

USC and Mom had both told me once I got my luggage I was to flag down a cab and go straight to USC. After two freeways and miles of palm trees, I finally arrived at USC. When the cab driver asked for sixty dollars, I blinked, and handed it over to him. I was lucky I had some cash from my high school graduation. I never thought about what a cab might cost.

It was the first time I'd ever even thought about money.

After paying the driver, I turned around and surveyed what was to be my new home for the next several years. I was now a USC football player and I thought, welcome to the good life.

Wearing a giant smile on my face, I rolled my two bags up to the football office. I saw a few of my new teammates who were upper-classmen. I nodded my head at them as if to say, "What's up?"

I continued on to the football office where one coach greeted me with a smile. My beaming face must have given him a clue because he paused and instantly turned serious. "Thomas, how was your flight? Good! Recruiting is over, it's time to get to work," he chuckled and walked away. "

I felt instantly confused, what was that all about?

I was here.

I was the man they had wooed into coming to USC. I was a Parade All-American, a five-star recruit. I was the savior. Wasn't I? Hadn't they been the ones calling me? They had visited me at my high school, coming to my house and assuring my mom I was the best.

Wasn't I the star player they had been looking for?

Reality Check

What happened next set me straight, confirmation that recruitment was truly over.

As I went into the locker room to where I found my name on my locker, I saw a pile of grey clothes on the seat of my locker. I unfolded the T-shirt and shorts. Something was missing.

No Cardinal and Gold USC logo.

There had to be a mistake.

I figured they forgot I was coming today. No problem. It wasn't even the first day of practice yet. All I had to do was talk to the equipment manager who showed me those sweet jerseys on my recruiting trip.

I calmly walked down to the equipment room and in my most polite voice said, "Excuse me, I think you guys forgot to put my clothes in my locker."

As I handed the clothes to the guy in the equipment room, he gave a chuckle and said, "No. These are yours all right."

"There's no USC logo. They can't be mine."

"They're yours, most definitely. You might be on the team, and you're going to practice on the USC field, but before you get the USC logo, you must earn the right to wear the USC logo. We don't give anything. You must earn everything."

As he spoke, I could even hear my mom's voice in my head, "Thomas, you don't get what you want in life. You get what you earn."

The equipment man confirmed it, "Until you earn the USC link, a plain grey t-shirt is what you will be wearing."

I thought, that's what I'd done the last four years. Coach Carroll had come to my school, called me personally, and now I had to *earn* the logo?

Something told me things were different than I'd expected. Before I knew it, things were only going to get more uncomfortable.

But before all that, I returned to my locker with my grey workout clothes without a logo. I'd dreamed about this day for most of my life, and somehow it wasn't turning out quite the way I'd expected.

I thought because I was on campus I deserved the jersey, that I'd jump right into the brotherhood of USC football, the players as happy to see me as I was to be there; the coaches slapping me on the back, big smiles on their face because we all knew I was going to be the reason for winning a Rose Bowl Championship.

Right?

No one else seemed to be part of the vision I had in my head. Recruiting was over and it felt like no fun to me. The clothes that were mine didn't have the USC logo on them. I had never before gone from the highest feeling to the lowest feeling in such a short time.

This was a huge letdown, I had no idea how to handle it.

Where Do I Sleep?

I had graduated high school only two weeks before, and now I found myself on the USC campus in the middle of the summer. The only people I was familiar with were the coaches who had recruited me from Vacaville High.

Today I felt invisible.

After a while, they informed me I would be rooming with upper-classmen until fall classes began and my scholarship actually started. I met the guys I was going to be staying with and as we walked over to the house where they lived, I carried my own gear and wondered what the next eight weeks were going to be like.

As an only child, I had grown accustomed to having my own room. I was really hoping I would at least get a room to myself. Not only did I *not* get my own room . . . I didn't even get a bedroom.

"That's where you'll be sleeping," said one guy.

I looked where he pointed.

The couch?

I was sleeping on the couch for the next two months? Seriously?

One look at the giant TV in the living room told me I would be pretty sleep deprived by the time fall semester started. That night, once they had finally shut off the television, I tossed and turned on the lumpy couch. The chop-chop-chop of low-flying helicopters searching for criminals didn't do much to help me to get a good night's rest either. That first morning I woke up at USC, I was as bleary-eyed and lethargic as if I had been up all night.

Didn't matter.

Time to head to school for my first training session with the team.

After putting on my non-logo clothes, I followed the other freshmen players along with the rest of the team feeling a little more optimistic than I had the day before. We were instructed to head into the weight room to get our body measurements. The strength coach told us once we were done to head out to the field to warm up.

Warm up? For what? Have you ever seen a dog warm up before it chases a cat? I was totally up for that. I wondered why we didn't warm up here inside of the weight room.

How hard could it be?

But we didn't just warm up. We broke up into five stations and a really quick observation told me this was unlike any "warm-up" I'd ever experienced in my life.

This wasn't just a warmup, this was a workout.

When I first arrived on campus as a scholarship athlete, I figured all the hard work was behind me. My first experiences with the team told me that the work was only just beginning.

Questions:

Think back to your first day on campus. You had intentions, aspirations, and long-term goals.

Write down 2 long-term goals you have for yourself (athletically):

1.
_____

_____

2.
_____

_____

Write down 2 long-term goals you have for yourself (academically):

1.

_____

_____

2.

_____

_____

What are 2 team goals you have for this season?

1.

_____

_____

2.

_____

_____

What are 2 personal goals you have for yourself this season?

1.

_____

_____

2.

_____

_____

From high school to college, what were some of the challenges you faced academically?

_____

_____

_____

From high school to college, what were some of the challenges you faced athletically?

_____

_____

_____

Just because you arrive, doesn't mean you've made it. The more you can define your goals, the more obvious the challenges are.

Identifying challenges allows you to create a game plan to overcome obstacles.

CHAPTER 3

Sick and Tired . . . of Being Sick and Tired

Small Fish, Big Pond

My first year as a USC Trojan forced me to take a really, *really* good look at myself. When I arrived that summer, I expected to be *the* player to take the team to a National Championship. USC *did* go to a National Championship that year, and we won the Rose Bowl.

In my dreams, I would have been at the head of the list of players responsible for that.

In reality, I watched my teammates from the bench.

I didn't play.

Was it that I wasn't good enough, I wasn't dedicated enough, I wasn't talented enough? It could have been.

Here's the reality; every single player recruited to play at the college level *is* good, dedicated, and talented. Sometimes there are others who are *better* than us in some way and they are in the starting lineup.

I knew that almost right away. My first year in college, I was not coachable. I hated when I was criticized about my efforts and athletic abilities. I had never been coached about my abilities back in high school, so I took coaching as criticism at USC. In high school, I could do whatever I wanted. It usually worked out. Like many high school athletes, all of us playing at the college level were the best of the best on our high school teams.

Once I got to USC, I was a little fish in a big pond. Coming from a small town, I was very uncomfortable with being that small fish.

For the first time in my athletic career, I allowed my emotions to get the best of me. One day after a particularly difficult practice, I went high up in the bleachers that overlooked the track where no one could overhear. I did something I never thought I'd do.

I called my mom.

"How is it? What's it like? Are you having fun?" Mom's voice came across the line, excited and full of anticipation.

I hated to throw water on her celebration, but I couldn't stop the tears that started right then. "I don't want to play anymore. I want to quit and come home."

Mom said nothing at first.

Usually I told her everything was great and I was having the time of my life. This time, I felt as though I couldn't stand one more day of practice, one more day of being coached hard.

When she did finally speak, I didn't like what she had to say.

"Thomas, it might take us a while to understand something, but once we got it, we never forget it. If you study hard enough, you'll get it. You practice hard enough, you'll get it."

What?

This answer did not give me the love and comfort I wanted. She didn't give me a way out. She forced me to face the lion. And it's the answer I needed. I got off the phone and trudged back for more torment. Her words echoed in my mind. Just because it's difficult now doesn't mean it will be like this forever.

Change Happens When . . .

You decide what you've been doing isn't working any more.

I had everything I needed to be successful. I was at USC on a full scholarship. I had a mom and a dad who both supported me in their own unique ways. I got really lucky as a freshman with a roommate who became a great role model for me and is still a great friend today, Reggie. It was somewhat accidentally on purpose that we ended up rooming together. We had met the previous year at the U.S. Army All-American Bowl, and I figured I'd like to room with someone I'd at least met before instead of a total stranger. This guy was quiet, hard-working, and he loved football as much as anyone I had ever met.

It didn't take long for me to realize this guy outworked every single one of the freshmen in our class, including me. The night before the first day of training camp, we were both studying our playbooks and training schedule. The playbook was as big as a telephone book. Reggie sat on his side of the room, I sat on mine, and after thirty minutes, I snapped mine shut. The information in the book seemed like a foreign language to me. I'd never studied a playbook before, I didn't know *how* to study a playbook. I was naturally better than other high school players and had relied purely on my raw talent to get me this far. Reggie stopped studying while we talked, and as soon as I was done asking questions, he put his nose right back in his playbook.

Right there was the dividing line.

I thought I was good enough, I had arrived and didn't have to work any harder. I felt like I had made it.

But Reggie didn't, and it showed. He always worked out harder, studied the playbook more intensely, and it was evident Reggie never stopped reaching for that ultimate goal, whether it was an A on a test, more reps in the weight room than the day before, or always coming in first during wind-sprints. Reggie was never satisfied with his performance. He constantly worked on getting better.

His example showed me I didn't know everything.

Reggie had bigger ideas. Reggie had specific and nearly impossible goals. He knew exactly where he was going and knew the exact steps he needed to take.

Usually you have to find the blueprint, the secret recipe, but here I was living with the epitome. I had the secret code living under the same roof and didn't realize it. My roommate taught me to think big and dream bigger, and to never lose sight that there is always more work to be done.

When I Was Fed Up

In life, we sometimes have to reach the lowest point possible before we say "enough is enough" and something has to change. That point came for me when we won the Rose Bowl against Michigan and named co-National Champions. After a trip to the White House where we had met President George Bush, we boarded a plane to LA. All the way back, I sat and listened to other players talk about winning another National Championship next year.

How can I do something again, if I haven't really done it at all? I hadn't played. I had nothing to do with winning that National Championship. I had been on the bench, watching them win.

There and then, I made a decision.

I had to be part of it next year.

Most of the time I pretended it didn't bother me. Now it was time for things to change. I had to take ownership of the problem and figure out the solution. It wasn't the fault of my coaches. It wasn't my teammates' problem. My issues were with myself.

The time had come when I got tired of being a spectator and wanted to participate. I went from being content with just being on the team, to wanting to *play* on Game Day.

Sick and tired of being sick and tired came for me when I was no longer happy just to have a jersey. I had watched, supported, and cheered my teammates long enough. It was time for me to figure out a way to get on the field.

How do we do that?

It all starts with a decision. You make up your mind and say, "Enough." For me, I began the offseason with a new mentality. I created a daily schedule that allowed me to maximize every single second of every day. I woke early, lifted weights, went to class, watched film of our games and our opponents, went to study hall, and did not go out during the week. I was committed to my goal of playing next season.

I learned to ask questions and really listen to the answers. One of my coaches, Ken Norton Jr., noticed my increased efforts and gave me some advice I treasure to this day. "You want to be noticed, Thomas? Then do something no one else is doing. I know you want to play defense. Until you do something to stand out, you will remain second string."

What could I do?

I figured how to use my frustration to my advantage.

My frustration fueled me.

Every time I felt I wasn't getting as much playing time I wanted, I used that frustration to drive me. It became my motivation. I set out to make sure I would not watch another game from the sidelines. My team was having too much fun and I wanted to be a part of it.

Whatever you need to do to increase your playing time, do it. If you need to get stronger, spend more time eating and get in the weight room. If you need to get smarter, talk to your coach, spend more time watching film.

For me, I had to focus on special teams.

It sounds special enough, doesn't it? In reality, nobody wanted to be on special teams. You play one play. You either kick off, receive a kick-off, or a punt. You have maybe thirty seconds on the field, and then you trot off and let offence or defense take the field. Why did I do that? For the exact reason my coach said, I intended to set myself apart. I became a wild, crazy, aggressive Hitman every second I was on the field. I shouted encouragement, I sweated determination, and I exuded confidence and belief that I was the best player on the field.

Even if it *was* for only thirty seconds. You become who you believe you are.

Did it work?

After being named "The Hitman" by Pete Carroll and a five-year NFL career, I'd say being sick and tired of being sick and tired is exactly what allowed me to maximize my career.

Whatever it takes, do it. Take charge of your career and *make* a role for yourself on the team and in the world.

Questions:

Big picture thinking: It is important for you to understand that where you are is only temporary, not permanent!

Describe the ideal role for yourself on your team:

_____

_____

If that is not your role now, what can you do every day that will help you achieve that?

_____

_____

_____

_____

_____

If you're already in that role, what can you do to take that role to the next level?

_____

_____

_____

_____

_____

_____

What sacrifices will you make to achieve greatness? Write down three things you are willing to sacrifice temporarily to get what you want in the future.

1.

_____

_____

2.

_____

_____

3.

_____

_____

Write down 3 things you know you need to work on as an athlete:

1.

_____

_____

2.

_____

_____

3.

_____

_____

We can learn something from everyone around us. What teammate do you admire in the way they approach their game?

_____

_____

_____

What do they do that makes you want to model their game?

_____

_____

_____

_____

_____

In order to get what we never had, we must be willing to do the things we have never done before to get it.

PART II

BECOMING A MAN

Note: I use the term "man" throughout this book because that is my perspective. I recognize a number of readers are likely female athletes. I apologize in advance for using this term, but it's the only way I know how to be. Please understand, I mean no disrespect. Interpret as necessary for your situation.

CHAPTER 4

Asking For Help

The Real Definition of Naivety

One of my coaches at USC used to tell us, "Be humble or you will be humbled." He would say this each time he sensed some type of arrogance from his players.

Is this really a problem?

I don't like to be the bearer of bad news, but the truth is yes, pride can be a problem. It's all about our ego and most of the time it gets it gets in our way, big time. When I arrived at USC, I was full of whatever it is you want to call it, pride, ego, or merely being full of myself. To me, I had reached the summit of my mountain. What I didn't realize about that mountain is it was the beginning of a new set of mountains I had to climb.

Initially, I figured I had whatever it took to get me where I needed to be. I'd gotten to USC on my own, hadn't I? Remember, I'm talking from my eighteen-year-old self, the one who thought I was the only reason I was where I was. This is where pride became a problem for me. It blinded me to the efforts of other people who helped me to reach my goal.

And this thinking continued to keep me further away from where I wanted to be.

I discovered the biggest problem with pride is I believed the only person I could trust and turn to in times of trouble or need was myself. Sound familiar? If so, please read carefully, because what you don't know really *can* hurt you! Playing sports, we often become prideful, sometimes to the point of not speaking up when we need or want something. We are taught to be the best on the field. We are called to be Superman.

When coach says, "You okay?"

We answer, "Yes!" without hesitation.

When coach asks, "Do you understand?"

"Yes!" Again, we answer without hesitation, without second thought because we are afraid of being seen as inadequate. On the court or on the field, we believe vulnerability is a sign of weakness, and we all know what happens then. That weak link is where the chain will break, and as athletes, we are determined to *not* be that weak link. Even when we cannot do something, we pretend we can.

As athletes, we know one thing: *Only the strong survive.*

And yet, how can we remain strong if we don't ask for help when we need it? It's really a fine line, isn't it, between being self-reliant and asking for assistance when we need it.

Here's the key . . .

. . . when you need help, *ask!*

I don't care if it's on the field, in the classroom, or in life . . . get the help you need by asking for it. If you're in the classroom and you don't understand the class material or an assignment, there is no shame in asking for clarification. How about when you're feeling really overwhelmed and you believe no one in the world understands what you're going through? Asking for help can be really beneficial, whether it is from a coach, a school counselor, or a mental health specialist. Asking for help is *not* a sign of weakness. In fact, it is one of the greatest signs of strength to recognize when you need help and you ask for it.

Not asking for help when you need it is the quickest way to failure I know.

Pride Goes Before the Fall

When I started classes the fall of my first year at USC I figured I would quickly and easily transition from being a high school senior to a college freshman. On the outside, I looked pretty successful. Hey, I found my classrooms, I was on time (mostly) in the beginning, and I sat with the rest of my classmates and tried to look like I was paying attention. It didn't take much time for me to know I was an imposter, at least in the classroom. The first day of class when the professor talked about office hours and to find what we needed on the syllabus, I was going, *sylla-what?* I was *not* going to raise my hand and prove to everyone else in the classroom I was clueless.

Not me.

And that kept going. For those of you who are in college, you know what that means. I was falling behind faster than anyone could have thought possible. I was at USC to play football and the classwork was the only way I would stay eligible. In my mind it was a necessary evil. But I wasn't keeping up. I didn't care about oceanography. Why pay attention? I didn't believe I would *ever* need to use that knowledge in my future. Believing my future to be the NFL, the idea of memorizing facts and figures about things swimming in the sea was a waste of my time.

Until I got to the point where I was in jeopardy of failing my classes. I needed help, and fast.

What to do?

Help!

Denise, my academic advisor at the time, suggested I take advantage of the TA for the class and her office hours.

Oh, I know what you're thinking . . . I was there too.

Me?

Ask for help?

I didn't want to look like an idiot. What I didn't realize at the time was *not* asking for help made me look exactly like I didn't want to look. Like a dumb jock. I did not want to reinforce the stigma that jocks are stupid.

Once I finally worked up enough courage, I went to the Teacher's Assistant office during her posted office hours. I resisted because I figured I'd have to wait in line while all the other people who weren't doing well in class to get all their questions answered first. I was *not* looking forward to the experience, but I knew if I didn't pull my grade up, I was in danger of losing my scholarship.

So I went.

To my surprise, there was no one waiting outside her office.

Had I gotten it wrong? Maybe she wasn't there. Maybe I misunderstood the time. When I knocked on her door, she looked up at me, smiled and said, "Come on in. How can I help you?"

Call me shocked. Was there really no one else in front of me?

At this moment, I began to understanding the element of pride. I wasn't the only one who suffered from it. There were other students in my class who were struggling, but I was the only one that day to seek the TA's help.

The first time, I was really uneasy. I mean, why should she help me? Who was I to her that she should spend her time explaining the concepts I didn't understand in class? But, since my eligibility was in jeopardy, I made the decision to go to her office every single week and realized she not only was there to help me, but she actually *wanted* to help me and see me succeed. Think about it, it's much easier for a professor to grade an A paper than it is for them to grade a paper with a bunch of mistakes. She even went so far as to explain to me how I could be even more successful in class by reading the material ahead of time.

Don't get the wrong idea.

She didn't spoon-feed me the answers. She taught me how to study, not only in that class, but in all my classes. She saw my determination to become a better student in her class and gave me every opportunity to be successful. That would have never happened if I hadn't shut my pride away in a suitcase and put it at the back of a very dark closet where it belonged. My TA helped with the material during her office hours. When it came time for class and passing tests, I understood the material because of all that extra time I put in when I went to her office hours.

When we don't keep our pride in check, it has the power to set us up for failure.

The faster you understand something, the more you can learn. Getting help is not a sign of weakness. Instead, it is a sign of strength. Even more importantly, it is a true strength because in vulnerability is true strength. Once I applied this knowledge about pride and pushing it aside to ask for help, I began to understand the road to success both in the classroom and on the football field.

Same concept with football. Not just, I went to practice and meetings the whole defense and offense went to, I should be good to go. Instead, I had to find it in my schedule to make it a point to see my coaches.

Don't understand how to watch film?

Ask your coach.

Coaches get paid to win games. If you don't know something, ask! The more you understand your game plan, the better your chances are to win.

Apply the same technique to your responsibilities as students.

Don't be afraid to ask!

If You Don't Know, You Don't Know

I once read an interview between Kobe Bryant and Bloomberg's Jon Erlichman in "Business Insider" where Kobe talked about his approach to entering the business world.

Erlichman asked Kobe, "What is this Kobe process? You'll pick up the phone and call people who are leaders in a certain industry and you'll pick their brain?"

Kobe said, "Absolutely!"

That's exactly what he does. He admits he could ask questions that might be really simple and basic for them, but as Kobe put it, "If I don't know, I don't know. You have to ask. I'll do just that."

If the great Kobe Bryant can humble himself to ask simple questions, why can't we do the same? The only way to get better at whatever you are doing, in class, on the court or on the field, is to ask questions. No one expects you to have all the answers. But, believe me, your coaches sure want you to ask questions if you don't know something. It's better to ask a question in the film room or during practice than it is to make a costly error in the game. You never know what benefits you'll get from asking questions.

Asking questions is what will take you to the next level.

Questions:

In your opinion, why is it so hard to ask for help when we need it?

Where do you feel most comfortable asking for help?

_____

_____

_____

List one place you can ask for help in these areas:

Athletically:

_____

_____

Academically:

_____

_____

If TAs (teacher assistants) and professors have office hours, how can you make time to see them every week?

_____

_____

_____

If coaches spend countless hours in their offices, how can you make time to see them every week?

_____

_____

_____

_____

_____

Pride and confidence makes you an elite athlete. It can be a gift and a curse when dealing with issues where we may need to get advice or assistance from others.

CHAPTER 5

Adversity – Academic Obstacles and the Injury Bug

Academic Obstacles

Going from a high school student at Vacaville High to a freshman at USC was a huge step in my life. For plenty of people, going to college is a norm. In my family, it wasn't as clear. I had an incredible dream once I set foot on the USC campus, and the dream was while I was the first in my family to go to college, I wouldn't be the last in my family to graduate from a university. I got into USC on an athletic scholarship, and all the people I met during my years at USC showed me a college education was like a magic key to life's possibilities. Over and over again I heard, "The more education you have, the more opportunities you will have."

Sure, I loved being a USC athlete, but getting a college degree was even more important to me.

It was NOT easy! As I shared with you previously, I had to learn to ask for help. The more important part of this chapter is for every college student athlete to understand the rigors of dealing with both the demands of sports *and* academics is a huge challenge.

It may very well be the biggest challenge we face as athletes.

In my case, I saw USC as the next step on my journey as I continued to the NFL. What I learned once I got there stunned me. When I was young and immature, I wanted to blame everyone else for academic challenges. I could blame almost anyone and anything. The truth is I had no one to blame except myself. My mom, my dad, my high school teachers, and coaches all supported me. It wasn't their fault I felt overwhelmed when I arrived as a freshman.

Years of conversations with current and former student athletes around the country, I've learned many people feel out of place during their first year in college. They may have been a good student in their high school in their hometown, but once they get to college, they're in a totally different environment. In college, you're competing with some of the smartest students in the country, students who come to school and know exactly why they are there.

They intend to get an education and define their own career path.

I'm almost ashamed to admit it, but the education was secondary, at best. When I first started at USC, I had it in my mind I was an athlete first and a student second. It didn't take me long to realize no one was going to hold my hand and get me through my classes. I had the responsibility of doing whatever it took to get the job done. Once I made that decision, quitting was not an option.

The only other option was to face reality. The reality is college curriculums are difficult.

Understand that and embrace it.

Pretty Smart for an Athlete

One of my biggest pet peeves was when I worked on a group project for one of my classes and I'd come up with a good idea. One of my classmates would say, "You're pretty smart," which had me smiling until they finished, "for a football player."

That always stung me.

I could never understand why athletes are seen as stupid jocks. Some of my favorite professional athletes are now business owners and no one would call them a dumb jock. Some of my very own teammates have gone on to their own successful NFL careers and are now in the world of business and finance. The biggest mistake any student athlete can make is to think they have to choose between being a good student or a good athlete.

The secret is this, you don't have to. Whoever said you can't be both?

I faced plenty of obstacles in the classroom during my years at USC. The upcoming chapters will outline how I managed to leverage time, resources, and my own intelligence to figure things out. The interesting thing is what worked for me on the field often worked for me in the classroom as well.

The Injury Bug

Injuries are a part of the game. It comes with being an athlete.

As athletes, we think we are invincible, we will never get injured...until we get injured.

Hear me when I say this, an injury is not the be all, end all.

An injury is a minor setback for a major comeback. During the time you are injured, you get to work on other parts of your game you may have neglected before. For example, if your leg is injured, you get to work on the mental part of your game. If a part of your upper body is injured, you can work on your lower body while your injury heals.

One part of your game might be limited, yet another part of your game can be conditioned.

There will come a point in your career when you will not be as fast as you once were, not as strong as you used to be, but you can condition your mind to become stronger. When you get injured, look at it as an opportunity to enhance other parts of your body that will come into handy later on down the road.

Working While Injured

As athletes, we're constantly reminded, "Take care of the body . . . you only get one body."

The game of football is violent. People get hurt on the field. We all hope and pray we dodge the injury bullet, and until it actually happens, we think, *it will never happen to me.*

I had my first injury as a freshman.

It was a minor knee injury during the Cal-Berkley game. But, it was an injury that required surgery. The same year I had to have a pelvic floor repair to reattach my groin on both sides. Yes, it's as painful as it sounds. The stupid part is I knew I had a twinge in my groin earlier in the year, during training camp, yet I still continued to play on it. Until I couldn't. I had to have mesh surgery and missed six weeks of training where all I could do was stretch and massage.

I had never had a real injury before college. Little tweaks and nags here and there, yet I had always been able to power through them like we all do.

When you rip and tear muscles, tendons, and ligaments, you're looking at surgical repairs, which sometimes mean long periods of recovery. My injuries drove home the concept that in the blink of an eye, in the three or four seconds it takes to make a play, the game can be taken away in an instant.

Our time in college is limited, specifically for student athletes. If you come in to college as a freshman, you have five years to use your four years of athletic ability. That additional year is for the usage of a redshirt.

For me, when I got injured, my playing time as an athlete had been put on hold, but my time at USC kept ticking. Not only was the clock ticking for me, when I got injured, it meant I got replaced. The party continued right along without me. The attention I once had was no longer mine. It belonged to the player who was available to play. Coaches no longer saw me as an asset. That was when I learned it was a privilege to play the game and I was not entitled to play.

I was dispensable!

That same year I missed the National Championship game versus Texas. Because of my injury, I was forced to watch from the sideline. Because of my injury and the fact that I couldn't play in the National Championship, I was mad. Depressed. And the worst thing of all, I couldn't help my team and I felt like I let them down.

The key here is don't wait for something to be taken away to appreciate it, because it may never come back. I learned very quickly that even while I was injured, I had to do everything I could to get back to 100% and do it fast.

Ken Norton, Jr. coached me well during this dark time. He told me to study more film to learn how to play smarter to make up for loss of my speed. He also taught me to learn several positions to give me more value to my current coaches and to my future NFL hopes. I had to learn to become versatile by learning to wear many hats. Ken Norton Jr. told me, "Thomas you're not *just* a middle linebacker or *just* an outside linebacker. You're a linebacker, period. Learn to play all linebacker positions."

Staying Mentally Strong

I might say athletes are some of the most physically developed humans on the planet. We build our bodies so we can push ourselves to do anything. We test our strength and then challenge ourselves to do more. Our bodies are big, strong, tough.

That's how we get results on game day.

The bigger game, however, is the one that is played between our ears.

What goes on in your head is what affects what happens on the field or on the court. How many times have you watched a championship game to see two well-matched teams go head to head, and in the 4th quarter there is a shift? One team is able to kick into another gear, leaving their opponent behind.

Physically, they're well matched.

But the mental game going on inside their heads is not so well matched.

Adversity hits every single athlete. Sometimes it's physical. Sometimes it's emotional. Sometimes it's purely psychological.

You can lose a game in your head before it's ever even played. At USC, we developed both physical and mental toughness. Mental toughness is not to be mistaken for stupidity, i.e. continuing to play while nursing a potentially severe injury. Mental toughness is all about blocking everything out of your head so you can be present during the moment.

Be where your feet are at all times.

When you're on the field, be on the field. When you're in the classroom, be in the classroom. Be prepared to do whatever it takes to overcome adversity in all forms in which it may show up.

In my mind, everything happens for a reason. The sum total of everything that has happened to you in the past results in the person you are today.

Trust me on this.

There is no fooling the person in the mirror.

As one of my coaches once challenged me, "How can anyone trust you to be there for them if you duck out when times get hard?" Be responsible and disciplined enough to do what has to be done, at exactly the moment you don't want to do it.

We might think the way we play sports is the way we live life.

But it's the other way around. Sports are fun. We want to do what it takes to be on the field.

The truth of the matter is this, the way we handle life, including life's adversities, is a much more accurate reflection of how we will play sports.

It's all fun and games when everything in your life is one hundred percent perfect.

But you have no idea what you're capable of until you're tested and challenged in the darkest of moments. By fighting your way through some adversity, you test YOU and discover exactly how strong you are mentally and physically.

The confidence you gain through adversity, the mental toughness you develop, is what makes you a MAN.

We become men, not by the plays we make on the field, but by the decisions we make off of it.

Questions:

What adversity have you faced?

Academically:

Athletically:

_____

_____

_____

_____

I learned the hard way that if I had implemented the following five game changers into my routine, my chances of being injured would have decreased dramatically:

- Ice tub
- Stretch
- Rehab

- Nutrition
- Proper rest

If you have ever missed playing time, what did you do to get back on the field?

_____

_____

_____

_____

_____

If you are injured, what other areas of your life can you focus on to fill the void?

_____

_____

_____

_____

_____

Don't let the things you can't do interfere with what you can do.

CHAPTER 6

Time Management

From the time you step on campus as a freshmen you have three, four, and at the most five years to accomplish everything you could possibly imagine.

You have practice, meetings, weights, rehab, class, tutor, study hall, etc.

This could all be overwhelming and the natural excuse is you don't have time to do everything. If you actually make a schedule outside of the demands you have with school and your sport you can actually accomplish everything you want in a single day.

In the same way your coaches devise a practice plan, you should also devise a plan for each day.

Every minute of your day can be accounted for.

From the time you wake up in the morning, to the time you go to sleep, there is enough time to maximize all of your day.

Tick, Tock – Time's Up

When I set out for USC, I knew I had a time limit, but seriously, on that first day, the only thing on my mind was I had made it. It never even occurred to me I had a limited amount of time to get everything done I wanted. I had achieved my biggest dream so far and for a long, long time, that was simply good enough.

What I didn't realize and what *most* student athletes fail to consider is while you're on an athletic scholarship, you have two jobs. Most people, who go to college, have one job only, to get an education. Student athletes have to be masters of time management or they will come up short and miss out on achieving everything that is possible.

If you don't produce on the field, the coaches will replace you. If you fail in the classroom, you've let yourself down, because the education that's being paid for by your scholarship is wasted *and* you find yourself no longer eligible to play. Many times, during my years, I heard the words, "This is the opportunity of a lifetime, make it count." At the time, the words disappeared in the wind.

Until one day, a coach chewed me out for getting a bad grade in one of my classes. "What are you going to do when you're academically ineligible? What then? Are you going to go to the games and sit in the stands and be *the guy who used to play football?* Are you going to go home and live on your mom's couch?"

His words stung.

Now I knew, this was the opportunity of a lifetime, I'd spent my whole life just getting here. The part I was missing, however, was I didn't have a single moment to waste. In the interest of full disclosure, I wasted plenty of moments. There were days when I wanted to sleep in, especially on days when my first class was all the way across campus and I didn't even like that class. I liked all of the attention I received on campus from the other students, especially the female students.

Who wouldn't enjoy being recognized as a student athlete?

From the time we step on to campus to the time our last day of school, there is a clock ticking and if we don't take advantage of the time we have the time we have will soon be gone and all we will ever have is, "shoulda, woulda, coulda."

No one wants to be that person.

When I didn't schedule my time, I found I didn't have very much of it. Once an hour or a day was gone, that was it. With my coach's words and those of my adviser echoing in my brain, I had to make a big change in how I approached both my academics and athletics.

I had to view my time at USC as an ever-dwindling bank balance, and I had to make the best use of every single minute of that precious asset. That was an account I couldn't overdraw.

Once the clock runs out, that's it. It's over.

There are no do-overs.

Don't Count the Time – Make the Time Count

The biggest concept I have learned about time is everyone gets the same twenty-four hours in the day. Some people count the time; other people make their time count. When you prioritize your time, you can accomplish twice as much as you would if you don't manage your time.

When I had trouble in class, I learned very quickly that spending time with the TA for that class during his or her office hours made my study time much more productive. I learned how to study and what to focus my study efforts on, rather than staring blankly at a book about a topic I didn't think I would ever use. When my academic adviser suggested I utilize my TA's office hours, she had handed me the keys to my academic success.

At first I wondered, why would I ever want to meet with my TA? And an even bigger question, why would my TA even want to meet me? My adviser told me by meeting with my TA, I could get help on the issues I struggled with in class.

She said, "Trust me, Thomas, your TA wants students to come in and ask them questions." She also gave me another tidbit of advice we will talk about more in the next section of the book. She told me to be sure to ask about the TA about their life outside of class. Show a personal interest in him or her.

Building a relationship meant much, much more than saying hello and goodbye. By taking the time to build rapport with TAs throughout your college years, you fully understand how important five or ten minutes of conversation can be.

Yes, There IS Enough Time

Scheduling visits to see my TAs was not easy. I had to create a daily calendar and find times where I could meet them. I put it in my calendar as carefully as I put dates and times of upcoming special practices and games. Learning this tool, scheduling all my time, I became much more efficient as a student. What was even more eye opening is I found I had more time to study film of our opponents so I could prepare for upcoming games.

This kind of extra effort gets noticed.

Just as my TA was more willing to give me the benefit of the doubt, my coaches also started to see my individual efforts and not simply another number on a jersey.

You can find time in your day to accomplish all of your daily goals. Seeing professors between classes allows you to get answers you couldn't get during lectures.

You need clarification on a specific assignment or your upcoming opponent? All you need to do is see your coaches to get your questions answered, so you will be able to confidently perform on game day. By having time management awareness and a system, you will be more productive so you can maximize your time and efforts.

Questions:

Take your 24-hour day and make an honest evaluation of how you spend every fifteen-minute period. There are programs on computers that can tell you what you spend time on. This is especially good if you think you spent four hours writing up a lab report, but when you look at the time summary you see you actually only spent about seventeen minutes on it. You spent the rest of those three-plus hours on social media, surfing the web, Skyping with friends, etc.

Write down your schedule for an average day during the season: (Practice, film, class, study hall, tutors, social media, etc. . . . and don't forget proper rest and nutrition can prevent injury. Schedule those!)

Wake Up:

Lights Out:

Write down your schedule for an average day during your offseason:

Wake Up:

_____

_____

_____

_____

_____

_____

_____

_____

_____

_____

_____

_____

_____

_____

Lights Out:

Now that you know what your entire day looks like, what are your biggest time-wasters? Talking with friends, Instagram, phone calls, and video games are not necessarily a time wasters, but unless something results from the time spent doing these things, you might want to protect those precious minutes.

Make a list of your top 5 time wasters.

1.

2.

3.

4.

5.

Everyone gets the same twenty-four hours in a day.

How you use your twenty-four hours determines what you accomplish each and every single day!

CHAPTER 7

Showing Up

80% of Success is Showing Up

When you show up, especially when it isn't mandatory, you set yourself apart from the rest of the crowd. By showing up, it means you care, and that's really important to people. They like to know you value their time so much you've decided to make time for them. In the case of my TA, by showing up at office hours as I had planned, I demonstrated a desire to improve my performance in that class. Since I was showing up for my TA, my TA showed up for me.

The very first time I did show up for the TA's office hours, I was a few minutes late. I thought, oh great, now I have to wait in line to get my questions answered. To my surprise, when I arrived, there was no one there. I entered an empty classroom where the TA sat typing on a computer. She was actually doing her homework for her graduate courses because no one was there.

I found out later, most of the time, no one *ever* showed up for office hours.

That right there was a huge advantage.

By showing up to a TA's office hours, I set myself apart from the rest of the class. I showed determination to improve my grade and I humbled myself enough to ask for help. By knowing I could attend the weekly office hours, it was easier to write down questions about things I didn't understand during the lectures and labs. The more questions I got answered during office hours, the better I understood the material.

One day, I decided to ask why she was willing to help me. Her answer shocked me. She said, "Thomas, I understand how hard you and your teammates work. I know how tired you all are when you come to class. You're trying as hard as you can, and by showing up at my office hours, you deserve to get your questions answered. Every single student in your class has the same opportunity to come to my office hours, yet no one does. Every week you're here putting in extra work and you deserve to be rewarded for it."

I want to share some valuable tips with you:

- Your professors and TAs have no way to know who you are. To them you're simply a number on a piece of paper, *until* you set yourself apart by showing up and putting in extra effort.
- As an athlete, you separate yourself from other athletes in your class by going to office hours and getting your questions answered. Saying hello and goodbye every day in class isn't enough.

- A short twenty-minute meeting can go a long way toward developing rapport and setting yourself apart from other students because you're now a name with a face and a personality.

- Campus resources are there for you, but they're not going to come running toward you. You have to ask for help when you need it, you have to find out when your professor or the TA has office hours to help. Most campus resources are grossly underutilized. Use that to your advantage.

- The most important person in your class is not the professor. It's usually the TA. The TA is the one who grades the papers and reviews the tests and exams.

Showing Up Yields Surprising Results

Showing up works in other areas too. When I talked to one of my coaches, asking how I can get on the field, I got an interesting piece of advice.

Focus on special teams.

Special teams might sound special, but the truth of the matter is no one really wants to be on special teams. You only get a couple of minutes on the field for one play.

Who was I to argue? I wanted playing time and if focusing on special teams might make a difference, then I would focus on special teams. Not only did I focus on special teams, I gave it all I had. I spent extra time with the Special Teams coach. I learned every play there was to learn. I learned multiple positions. I spent a lot of extra time viewing film of upcoming opponents in order to be the special teams expert for an upcoming game. Every practice, I went on the field with all the enthusiasm as though it was the most important play ever. I played special teams as though it would change the outcome of the game.

That kind of showing up got me noticed. The increased exposure got me the recognition to get put on defense, which got me playing time. My increased efforts, hard practice, and preparation for special teams were all about me showing up. Showing up takes absolutely no ability. It only requires a relentless effort on your part.

Extra Effort

Before anyone begins to think by showing up, all you have to do is be physically present. There must be effort as well. It's not enough to breathe the air and take up space. When we show up, that means with intent to succeed. That's when people see you as someone who cares about what happens. That extra effort often opens more doors than you thought possible.

Showing up to your professor in office hours, will lead to the benefit of the doubt when it comes time to grade. Showing up to your coach's office when it not mandatory demonstrates your sport is important to you. When you show up in study hall and study when it is not scheduled your academic advisors will go out of their way to help you. Showing up when it is not mandatory goes a long way. People take notice of who shows up when it is not mandatory. The ones who show up when it is not mandatory give themselves a better chance of being noticed, remembered, and being liked.

The more people who notice you, remember you, and like you the more opportunities will come your way.

Questions:

What are the benefits of showing up when it's not mandatory?

Academically:

Athletically:

List 2 places in your life you can show up more when it is not mandatory:

1.

2.

Showing up when it is not mandatory tells people:

- *That it is important to you.*
- *That you care about that person's time.*
- *That you are accountable.*

CHAPTER **8**

Taking Charge of Finances

Financial management is a skill set that keeps everyone, college athlete and professional athlete alike, in the black and out of the red. In order to get a professional perspective on this topic, I interviewed my fellow USC teammate, Jeff Byers.

Jeff was a highly recruited offensive lineman who got bit by the injury bug early in his USC football career. True to his nature, Jeff saw that not as a problem, but as an opportunity. Jeff's doctor told him he may never play football at the same level again. Discouraged and uncertain, Jeff turned to his father for guidance. His father suggested Jeff make full use of the USC resources available to him. Jeff learned, by talking to the head of academic resources and the dean of the business school, he could earn his undergraduate degree in three years and get his MBA in two years.

Jeff beat the injury bug and continued to play USC football. He went on to a four-year NFL career before retiring from football to be a financial adviser to some of the wealthiest people in the world. Jeff's advice is sound and critical to understand.

Your Scholarship is NOT Financial Security

While Jeff managed to turn his injuries into a bonus by earning his MBA while still under full athletic scholarship, he also managed to avoid the financial problems many college students experience. Because he worked through high school, Jeff arrived at USC with a tidy nest egg in his pocket. A nest egg that immediately saw withdrawals because Jeff's scholarship, as with most incoming student athletes, did not start until you've registered for classes. All too quickly, rent, gas, food, and other activities took their toll.

Every student on an athletic scholarship gets a monthly stipend. Jeff saw that as another opportunity. He made a monthly budget where he listed every single monthly expense he would have, and then make sure he didn't spend above his stipend amount. In fact, Jeff made a game of trying to save as much as possible from every stipend check.

According to one of the university's staff who disburses stipend checks, some student athletes get their check on the 26th of the month and are back in her office the 3rd or 4th of the next month asking for advance on their next check because they spent their stipend checks and now were behind on their rent.

Your stipend check won't allow you to live like a king, but it will give you a comfortable living. With it, you'll be able to rent an apartment with at least one roommate where you can split expenses. There should be enough for gas, your phone bill, and some food.

As I said, it's not enough to allow student athletes to live like royalty, but you'll have food, water, and shelter.

Money In, Money Out

I asked Jeff what the real secret to financial literacy might be. He said, "Know how much money you have coming in and how much is going out. Always make sure you have more coming in than going out." There are ways to ensure this. One is to make more money.

For some student athletes, this is certainly possible, especially during off-season. Sure, there is still training and sometimes summer school, but there is still time to have a job or an internship where you can earn a stipend and also other income as well check and have a little more cash on hand.

Financial guru, Warren Buffet, whose net worth is north of **65 BILLION** dollars, said, "Never depend on a single stream of income."

What happens when you can't take on another job? The only way to have a good balance in your account is to identify all of your expenses and eliminate anything that isn't necessary. If you do this from the very beginning, it becomes second nature. Some students, like Jeff, have a built-in cushion in that they arrived at college with extra money in their bank account from jobs they held during high school. It might take them a little longer to realize they're bleeding their account dry. The day will come when there are more expenses than money coming in. The only way to avoid that scenario is to know exactly what you're spending your money on.

Making a Budget

Do you know what your monthly expenses are?

I mean, do you *really* know what they are? In some of my seminars, I've asked student athletes to make a rough budget to see where their money goes and how much their stipend pays for. It surprised me when one of my students said, "Do I guess how much my phone bill is for this?"

In order to be on top of your finances you can never guess about anything. Jeff told me nearly every person he knows would *under*estimate how much they spend every month. This translates into not having enough money to pay bills before your next stipend check arrives.

One of the exercises at the end of this chapter is to have you make a personal budget. Take a moment to think about your monthly expenses.

Do you use credit cards? If so, get those statements out, I'm going to have you add any expenses you've put on credit to your budget. Because it's on a credit card doesn't mean it doesn't count. In fact, putting credit cards away for a time is a good way to slow down your spending while you figure out your budget.

Save all receipts, keep a notebook if you can't remember where you spent money last month. The idea is to build as complete an expense sheet as possible.

Next, you add up how much money you have coming in. You put in the amount of your stipend check and any other income you have from a job or internship.

Add both columns.

Subtract expenses from income.

If you end up with a negative number, this is a critical chapter for you to understand.

Do You Want it or Need it?

Regardless of your current situation, we can all improve our habits. For any of you who read my first book, *Permission to Dream*, you'll know I experienced some hardship as a kid. I always had food, water, and shelter. Some years there was more food than others. Most years, there wasn't enough money for me to buy the latest sports gear. If I wanted a jersey, Mom usually steered me toward last season's jersey. Last season's jersey was less expensive. Same for my shoes. In about every area of my life, we scrimped and saved to get by. When I arrived at USC on scholarship, I really did believe I had arrived. With my first stipend check, I felt rich. I went straight to the mall and I couldn't just get an outfit, I had to get a new pair of shoes what went with it.

After all, I deserved it, didn't I?

We all have a right to spend our money in any way we choose. In my conversation with Jeff, however, he told me of his very wealthy clients who are worth hundreds of millions of dollars and they still fly coach. Others could buy an entire town, and yet live in a modest neighborhood, drive an older model car and no one would know how wealthy they are. This lesson right here is a key to financial literacy. You can spend all of your money on things you want right now, or you can save some of that and spend money only on what you need for the moment.

Lawrence Jackson, who is a former USC teammate, asked me one time. "Would you rather be a cowboy with a big cowboy hat or a cowboy with a lot of cattle?

Would you rather appear to have a lot of money, or would you rather have a lot of money and not need to appear like you do?

Want.

Need.

What's the difference? A need is something essential to living. We need water, food, and shelter in order to survive. With my stipend check I needed to pay for rent, utilities, and groceries. Beyond that, most other expenses were not needs. I bought things because I wanted them. Some student athletes are good at making choices. Do I buy a new pair of shoes, or do I go out to dinner with friends? Both of these are probably wants, but by choosing between the two, you still wind up saving a bit of money. It's when you can't choose, can't determine if it's a want or a need that gets us into trouble. Usually when we aren't disciplined enough, we buy both wants and needs.

The True Value of Your Scholarship

The biggest lesson I learned is what my scholarship was truly worth.

At first, I figured it was my monthly stipend. That's what a lot of student athletes think. Our athletic scholarship is another huge opportunity. According to Jeff Byers, student athletes on scholarship are way ahead of the rest of the population because even if they never go pro, they are much wealthier because they graduate without enormous student loans.

Tuition and fees approximately $50,000 an academic year

Stipend for rent / other expenses $1800 a month over 9 months during the academic year (would get $450 a week for summer based on # of weeks of summer class)

Total value approx. $66,000 for academic year

If go to summer school add an additional $5,400 stipend for 12 weeks plus approximately $13,300 for 8 units of class work totaling $18,700 and you are looking at about $85,000 a year

Also add the benefit of the enhanced meals that all students now get which probably is worth $25 a day.

As an example, here is a sample of what an academic scholarship might be worth today at a private university:

The total value of the scholarship is approximately $66,000 per year. That's a great deal of money. Add in the extra summer school benefits and enhanced meals, you're looking at closer to $85,000 to $90,000.

In addition, that's *before* you consider all the benefits student athletes get in terms of free clothing in the form of shoes, shorts, sweats, shirts, etc. with their school's logo on them. When you travel to away games, around six times a year for football, you can add about $1,000 per away game to pay for chartered airplanes, chartered buses, five-star hotels, and per-diem for food.

That means your scholarship is really worth close to $100,000. This would be the same as if you had been paid $100,000 for the year.

10/10/10

Why is it important to understand how much the scholarship is worth?

Let's look at a few facts. While society has placed an incredible amount of importance and stigma on the value of being an athlete, your time as an athlete is limited. In 2008 at the rookie symposium, former NFL wide receiver and Hall of famer Chris Carter told us, you guys have now entered into the 10/10/10 parts of your career. Some of you will play football for the next 10 weeks (2-1/2 months) some of you will play for the next 10 months (one football season) and very few of you will play football for the next 10 years.

This rule serves as a reminder to show us how uncertain our athletic careers are. Professional sports are not like college. In college, you are guaranteed four or five years. In professional sports, there is no scholarship.

There are no guarantees.

We were told there are no guarantees you will be the one who will play for ten years. You might even play for a mere ten minutes, get injured to the point you are no longer valuable to the team and suddenly your career could be over before it even began.

In terms of percentages, approximately 99% of student athletes never go pro. Suddenly this puts things into perspective. Having a scholarship as a student athlete gives you an opportunity to get a college education and graduate debt-free. From there you can expect to find a job, and for most graduates, an entry-level position could be anywhere from $40,000 to $70,000, depending on your degree.

Sounds like a great deal of money, doesn't it? After all, you were living on a stipend of maybe $1500 to $1800 a month. Right? Not so fast. An annual salary of $40,000 is approximately $3,333 dollars a month. Take out for taxes and insurance, you're left with something pretty close to your stipend check. Only it won't feel like it because you no longer have free health insurance, free food, free clothing, and free 5-star hotel and luxury travel on chartered planes and buses.

Enjoy your time at college while on scholarship, but know it will come to an end. That is something I can guarantee 100%.

Only 1% of college student athletes go on to play professional sports.

But 100% of all athletes have to retire.

Then life continues, it will take a lot of effort to balance what money you make which is a completely new formula from when you were a college student athlete or pro-athlete.

Going Pro, I've Got It Made, Don't I?

I'd like to say sure, you absolutely have it made. Jeff brings his wisdom from his personal experience. For those who consider going pro before they get their degree, he reminds them it's really hard to go back to school after playing pro ball. In his mind, unless you're a first round draft pick, and you're lucky enough to play enough years to earn your full contract amount, you may never have to worry about money again.

But for everyone else, Jeff suggests you get your degree before going pro because no one can ever take your degree away from you.

Your professional career can end in the blink of an eye. Jeff sees sports as a microcosm of life, not a job or a career. "It's something you do because you love it. If you can leverage it so you make enough money to get you a great head start on the rest of your life, then use that opportunity. You have a limited time as an athlete. You have a lifetime as a person."

Whether you're a student athlete or a pro athlete, know your income and expenses. While you're still a student athlete, keep this in mind, every single month, on the same day, a scholarship athlete gets the same amount of money. Each year the amount increases, but inside of that there is a false sense of financial security. From the first check to the last check habits are formed. Most of the habits formed are not positive habits. When these bad habits are formed, that is when we run into problems. The problems cause us to spend above our means.

After four or five years of this behavior, habits can form. If we don't curb this in time, we face really big problems.

Understanding your annual cost of living will allow you to know exactly how much money you need to make when you leave college. Create good spending habits while you are in school so you can build wealth even before you go pro. Even if you have the opportunity to play pro sports, if you're financially illiterate with a little money, you will still be financially illiterate, only with a bigger bank account.

Know this . . . it is not about how much money you make, it's about how much money you keep.

Questions:

Take inventory:

What are your monthly needs?

_____

_____

_____

_____

_____

What are your monthly wants?

_____

_____

_____

_____

_____

Personal Budget:

Income – (How much do you make each month (stipend check, financial ad?)

_____ Stipend check

_____ Financial aid

_____ Offseason internship

_____ Other income (try to include everything)

_____ **Total Income**

Expenses – (How much do you spend each month?)

_____ Rent

_____ Utilities

_____ Phone bill

_____ Car payment (or transportation costs)

_____ Insurance

_____ Gas

_____ Food

_____ Haircut

_____ Clothing

_____ Entertainment (eating out, movies, hanging out
with friends)

_____ **Total Expenses**

How much do you have left over?

Or do you have any left over?

*Remember this: If you make fifty million and you spend fifty-one
million, you're broke.
It's not about how much you make, it's about how much you save.*

CHAPTER 9

Ownership

It's Up to YOU

You've heard the phrase, "The buck stops here," haven't you? When you say that, you become fully responsible for your actions. No blame game. No pointing fingers. Simply looking in the mirror to make the necessary changes to improve your situation. When a man says "I'm responsible," or "It's my fault," it means he's taking ownership of whatever the issue is and handles it.

I will be the first one to admit on many occasions, I looked for someone or something to blame. I didn't have the right equipment. It was raining. It was too hot. Someone tripped me. I didn't get enough sleep the night before. I wasn't ready. You name it, I came up with an excuse for it. As kids, we're really good at that because we don't ever want to be seen as not able to get something done.

When I finally realized the only person I had to blame for anything was myself, I began to make different choices in my life. That's when I went from just a kid in college to becoming a man.

If I chose to stay up late having a good time with my boys, then I had no one to blame but myself the next day at practice when coach decided to put me in with the first string and I couldn't hold my own because I didn't get enough sleep. My lack of production in school and on the field came from my poor decision-making.

When I overspent my stipend check and didn't have enough money to buy groceries the last week before getting paid again, I could only blame myself. I soon realized I couldn't eat a new outfit and a new pair of shoes that I chose to get over buying the groceries I needed.

Learning to stop the blame game and take ownership over my life meant I had to make better choices in all areas of my life. Sure, there are some things we like doing, but in the long-run, is that the best decision?

I'm not saying you can't have fun while you're in school. Far from it. What I'm saying is, the choices you make in life are what shapes the outcome. Once I started taking ownership for all my decision, I began to relax and have a lot *more* fun at school.

Why?

I had more fun because I didn't have any guilt or burden holding me down!

That's right. Taking ownership means when you make better choices, you know you have done your absolute best in every place in your life and when things go well, you can celebrate rather than know deep down you're celebrating on the outside, but on the inside you know you didn't have anything to do with that success. The best example of that was when I got sick and tired of being sick and tired. Yes, I was a USC football player my first year when we won the Rose Bowl. Yes, I celebrated with my teammates. Yet I hadn't played in the game. I had no field time. I did nothing to help my team win that championship. I felt like a poser. I got the glory, but deep down I knew I did nothing to deserve it.

There is no worse feeling than that.

Things Happen, What Will You Do About Them?

I used to think bad luck was simply that.

Bad luck.

When I got bit by the injury bug, I figured I'd gotten a bum deal. I didn't even think it was my fault. In retrospect, it was my fault. I knew I had pain I should have paid attention to and gotten a medical opinion on. But no, my arrogance told me, "Don't worry, you'll be fine. You don't want the coaches to know you're injured." Seems like good advice, until you suddenly really can no longer play. Then you're on the operating table and the football season marches right along without you, making you feel like you're a million miles away even when you're in the same locker room.

Jeff Byers got bit by the injury bug too, and even earlier in his career than I did. What did he do about it? He turned it into an opportunity to further his education while he was recovering. When he was able, he did rehab and recovery until he was back on the team and making plays. My roommate, Reggie also got bit by the injury bug, and he absolutely *chafed* at not being able to work out. The instant he was cleared for duty, he was full speed. He took off and was racking the weights at the earliest possible training time.

Watching my teammates taught me a lot about myself and the choices I made in my life. I had to ask myself a lot of hard questions. Am I living up to my full potential? Am I wasting the opportunity of a lifetime? Do I really want to cry and complain to my mom, to my girlfriend? Will their sympathy make my circumstances go away?

The only way to move ahead is to take ownership over every single aspect of your life.

I had to do it with mine, and it started with a really good look in the mirror. I've said it many times before, "There is no fooling the man in the mirror." You can say what you like to people. Only you know yourself better than anyone. You know when you're putting in your best effort and when you're blaming others or your circumstances for your failings.

Seriously, the buck MUST stop with you.

Because if it doesn't, then all you're doing is playing the blame game, hoping someone else is responsible for your problems, your mistakes, your bad choices.

Owning Your Time and Your Finances

It took me a very draining and difficult year to figure out unless I scheduled all my activities, including time with my TA and my coaches, I would fall so far behind I would never catch up. When my coach blew a gasket over my D in Oceanography, I admit to being perplexed at first. What did he care if I learned about Oceanography? I didn't think I would *ever* use that information in my lifetime.

His reaction was based *not* on how well I knew the material, but on whether I would be eligible to play for the team or not. I think it was at that moment I really understood the concept of consequences. If I chose not to study for my classes, I risked getting a failing grade which would make me ineligible to play ball. If I didn't play ball, USC would no longer pay for my education. It's really a simple business decision. This allowed me to understand the true concept of asset versus liability.

An asset adds to the team, assists the team, helps the team to win games. A liability is dead weight, no matter how optimistically you look at it. You can be an asset as an injured player as long as you show intent to come back and do your part for the team. The instant you demonstrate you no longer care about the team, you're dead weight and will get left behind. The last thing a student athlete wants is to be let go from the team because there goes the scholarship and all dreams of playing professional sports and the life you have always envisioned.

In essence, you have to position yourself as an asset in the eyes of your coaches. That means you have to manage your time, take care of your responsibilities and figure out how to maximize your schoolwork, time in your sport, and other priorities you have in life.

In terms of finances, unless I got a job or an internship, I had to live within my means. My scholarship gave me the opportunity to get an education, the first ever in my family to go to college. I didn't actually appreciate how important that was to my family until I talked with my dad. He told me there were many times he wanted to quit the military. It was hard. It was demanding. And it whooped his backside. Every single time he thought about quitting, he thought about me and how he wanted me to have the chance to have an education and a life he could only dream about.

I didn't know my dad very well until I started college. We lived apart for most of my growing up years. The one year I do remember living with him, he seemed to be a hard taskmaster, and a confused man trying to make sense out of life.

When I got to USC, my dad became my go-to guy for problems. My mom had given me every single opportunity and without her, I would have never made it to USC. Once there, I needed some sympathy. From Mom, I got tough love. From Dad, I got an ear to hear me and then reflect my words back. Even though my dad wasn't there when I thought I needed him the most, he was there when I actually *did* need him the most.

Becoming a man means learning what it takes to *be* a man. Dad told me he made plenty of mistakes, but when I had problems in college, Dad listened and gave counsel.

One thing he never did was allow me to blame someone else for my own personal failings.

I learned to be a man from my dad and from my coaches and from the other men surrounding the USC athletes.

I learned to accept responsibility for my actions.

I learned to make opportunity out of adversity.

In short, I learned how to own my life.

Questions:

Look in the mirror. What excuses have you used, blaming others where you could have owned up to the responsibility?

_____

_____

_____

_____

_____

Here are ways you can tell you are not taking responsibility for your life:

- *Blaming others*
- *Blaming circumstances*
- *Blaming past experiences*

Questions you can ask when you are taking ownership:

- *What can I do to fix the issue?*
- *What can I learn from this situation?*
- *What can I do in the future to avoid this from happening again?*

CHAPTER 10

Social Media – What is Your Brand?

Your Brand? Yes, You!

When we think of social media, we instantly think of Facebook or Instagram photos, or the rant you followed and chimed in on Twitter. That's all fun and games until it's time to really show up in the world. What image are you portraying for your followers?

After my the NFL career, I decided my passion was to continue working with athletes, specifically helping student athletes prepare for the step in their lives that takes them beyond the stage of being a college superstar. One of the biggest areas of focus inside of my work is the image student athletes put out there on their social media platforms.

Immediately after I retired, I met with a couple of advisors. One of the very first things they did was ask me to open up my Facebook to take a look at the kinds of things I posted, what I liked, and how I showed up on such a public platform. I didn't think I had any worries, but soon the frowns and glances between my advisors told me a different story.

They didn't come right out and judge me, rather they gently questioned me about certain photos. "When you see a photo of yourself at a party with a red Solo cup in your hand, what does that tell the viewer?"

"That I was having a good time." To be honest, I never thought about why I posted that photo or any photo for that matter.

"Or, you're a partier."

"And that's bad?" At first, I didn't get it. How could a photo of me having fun be a bad thing?

"No, not necessarily bad, but you might want to consider that some people who follow you could be young people who look up to you. They might model your behavior, they might be underage. The example you represent on your social media might say underage drinking is acceptable."

I sat back, stunned.

I thought my social media presence was the same as it was for everyone else; to share the fun or momentous occasions of my life, something to do when there's nothing to do. I'm bored, so "look at me!"

I wasn't really thinking, and followed the example of doing what I've seen others do. That mentality of social media can get you into trouble. Is your goal to get 100 likes? What happens when only get 99?

Social media is an unreal world.

It may appear other people have the perfect life. That's only because they've painted an illusion of their life. They only posted what they wanted others to see.

After my advisors explained all this to me, I realized I wanted to inspire and motivate the people who follow me or happen to be on my social media profile.

You are 100% in control of what you put in front of your viewer.

At that moment, I understood I was not just "Thomas the Football Player," I was "Thomas, The Brand."

A brand? What were they talking about?

Now I totally get it, and if there is only one thing you get out of this book, it should be this: As a student athlete, you have gone beyond the realm of being merely an anonymous student at a university. If anyone wants current or past information on you, it's right there at the tip of their fingers; your face, your behavior, and your performance. What goes on the web is there forever.

Someone's grandma used to say, "If you don't want to see it on the front page of a newspaper, you shouldn't be doing it."

The same goes for what we post on Facebook. If I wouldn't be comfortable enough saying it to my grandmother, I probably shouldn't post it. This is even true for the things we "like" on Facebook. If we regularly "like" off-color jokes, profane memes, or derogatory posts, we're sending that out to the world as though we posted it ourselves.

Today it might not matter.

But tomorrow, you will be sitting across the desk from a very powerful person who has your entire future right there on the desk. One glance at your social media presence could have the two of you shaking hands on the deal of a lifetime or you could be quietly and quickly escorted from the room, watching the next athlete ushered into the office, presented with the opportunity you just lost.

You have a name, a jersey, a number. Those seem to be a given. There were plenty of things that were never explained to me. I was much more than merely my name, my jersey, my number.

I was my brand.

And so are you.

Beyond "Likes" is Brand

When I do workshops, I always talk about social media because more than 90% of student athletes participate in it in some form or another. Did you know, if you wanted, you could actually set yourself up for a job or an internship, or if nothing else, a free pair of shoes if you properly utilize your social media platform?

One athlete I know absolutely loves Nike. Everything this student athlete put on had the Nike logo on it, and trust me, his social media showed it. He posted himself using Nike cleats, huge travel bags, shirts, gloves. You name it, he posted it. When he approached Nike for an internship, you know the first thing they checked?

You got it.

His social media presence.

And they saw he wasn't kidding about how much he loved their products. The proof was right there in front of them, on all his social media pages going back for at least four years that he supported them by wearing their brand in every way he could.

Did he get the internship?

Without question!

Who better to represent their brand than an athlete already marketing for them?

Social Media Etiquette

You must remember, for the outside world, there is no line drawn between who you are as an athlete and who you are as a person. You *are* more than a number on a jersey.

Here are three things to remember when dealing with social media:

1. **Keep the Locker Room in the Locker Room**

   By that I mean everything. Language. Tone. Style. Cursing. Everything. What you put out there on social media is for general consumption. It's an opportunity for you to explain who you are as a person, share your hobbies and interests, and to recognize you have fans. YOU HAVE A FOLLOWING! I don't care if you're the third string punter or the starting quarterback, YOUR BRAND belongs to you.

2. **No Emotional Outbursts on Social Media.**

   I know, you should have been playing but coach didn't put you in, you didn't agree with the play call at the end of the game, or someone in the stands criticized your last play. Stay away from social media at that point. Never respond emotionally to anything. No interactions with negative fan talk . . . how you got a raw deal and you want to tell your side of the story. You want people to side with you. The problem with venting on social media, once you press send, it's permanently out there.

3. **Build Your Team and Your Brand Up**

After Super Bowl 49 when the Seattle Seahawks lost a close game to the New England Patriots, Seattle Seahawks Quarterback Russell Wilson took to his social media to build his team up. Was he upset? I'm sure he was. Did he wish the outcome of the game had been different? Absolutely, but everything he posted following that game was positive. He addressed social media, talking about how that game was going to be motivation for him and his teammates, how they would become stronger the following season, and he was so proud of his team for the way they played all season long. Russell Wilson not only talked about his team in a positive light during what could have been a negative tweet or post, he also thanked the Seahawk fans, better known as the 12s, for supporting the team all season long.

How can you show the outside world there is another side to you? By being very aware of everything you post on social media. Not only will your fans be checking you out, but people offering internships, future employers, and professional coaches. Your potential endorsement deals ride on your brand and your social media presence. If your viewers don't like what they see, they'll never, ever contact you. That is free money you'll be leaving on the table.

Trust me, once it's out there, it's permanent. It will never disappear. Far better to clean up your social media profiles today, and keep them clean. That way you won't worry about what others might think about you. You can paint the picture you want your followers to see.

Here is an example of how much social media can affect you. Sean Covich is a golf coach at West Virginia. In his 150-character tweet, on January 6, 2016, he says it all:

> *Dear recruits: If I research your social media and find multiple uses of profanity/pics of alcohol, will likely cost you a scholarship.*

Questions:

Here are some social media platforms you might be using:

Facebook
Instagram
Twitter
Snapchat
LinkedIn
Pinterest

What are three reasons you use social media?

1.

2.

_____

_____

3.

_____

_____

When you post on social media, what is the image you want your followers to have of you?

_____

_____

_____

_____

_____

What issues, themes, or topics do you typically stay away from talking about on social media? Will you change your mind after reading this chapter?

_____

_____

_____

_____

_____

_____

What advice would you give younger athletes as it pertains to the use of social media when posting?

_____

_____

_____

_____

_____

Do you see how your social media presence can affect future job opportunities?

_____

How often do you interact with your fans and followers on social media?

_____

_____

_____

_____

_____

_____

The next time you're on social media, go back and look at your profile:

Make sure every single one of your photos and posts align with your brand, morals, and values.

PART III

LEGACY

CHAPTER 11

Giving Back

What Will Your Legacy Be?

We have talked so far about identity and working toward figuring out who you are and how to control that in different situations. We went on to learning about what it takes to be a man, taking responsibility, asking for help, managing resources, and keeping your word without excuses. All are necessary. Now let's move on to the next phase of this book: Shaping Your Legacy.

Your life is made up of moments you experience today. Legacy is what you leave behind; how you will be remembered.

Live for today with the end of your life in mind. Ask yourself the question: What will your 80-year-old self look like? One way of looking at it will be defined on what you accomplished. The other will be based on how you were able to positively affect the lives of others.

Life is much more than being an athlete. Your time as an athlete will come to an end. You will win games, you will lose games, hopefully more wins than losses.

Your time will be measured more by the way you treat other people.

On the football field, when I got to paint my face black and strap on my shoulder pads and go out on the field and inflict pain on opposing teams excited me. I will never forget the advice of one of my mentors in the Equipment Department gave me. Everyone called him Pops. For myself and many other student athletes at USC, Pops was like a father figure.

When Pops talked, we listened.

One day Pops turned to me and said, "Thomas, who won the Super Bowl five years ago?"

I had no idea.

"Who won the Super Bowl three years ago?"

I still didn't know.

"What about last year's Super Bowl?"

It took me a moment, then I finally remembered who won.

"You know why I'm making this point?"

"No, sir, I don't."

"I want you to remember this, wins are extremely important. But, you want to know what is more important than that?"

At the time, I thought, *what could possibly be more important than winning?*

"The way you affect people. What do people think when they see you walking towards them?

What do people say when you leave?

Do people get excited when they see you walking toward them? Or do they put their head down hoping you don't see them?"

I had never paid attention.

Pops went on, "How many points did Magic Johnson score during his basketball career?

Again, dead silence.

"What is Magic known for, today?"

I said, "For business, creating jobs and generating revenue for Urban America." I finally knew the answer to one of his questions.

He said, "Exactly!" But Pops wasn't done yet. "How many touchdowns did Jim Brown score?"

I had no clue.

"What is Jim Brown known for today?"

"For being a father figure to men and for his efforts in preventing gang violence and getting gang members to start loving instead of killing one another." I felt good knowing the answer to another question.

Then Pops asked me a zinger, "What about you, Thomas. What will you be remembered for? When the game stops for you, when you're no longer the Hitman, what will you be known for?" He took me out of the equipment room and he pointed to one of the janitors pushing a trash can. "Do you know that person's name? Do you ask them how they are doing? Do you try to leave them with a smile?"

He already knew I didn't know the person's name.

"Thomas," he said, "people are more important than touchdowns. You have to understand by smiling at them, asking them how their weekend went, these people's lives will ultimately be better. You don't know what they are going through at home or what happened on their way to the school this morning. With you taking a brief moment of your day, you have no idea how you can positively affect their day, leaving a lasting impression on their hearts." He went on, "No one asks these people how they're doing because they see them simply as the janitors. They might not be able to do anything big for you right now, but think about what they are doing for you all the time. You have clean bathrooms, your locker room is not dirty, and the hallways are clean. If you did not have them around, then you wouldn't have this clean facility."

He paused for a moment, then said, "I want you to think about how many people you pass by on a daily basis. How many smiles are out there that you are not uncovering? You never know how just your smile and acknowledgment will impact someone's day. Think about it, you're a USC football player and you have this aura about being an athlete. If you make time to ask people how they are doing and recognize them, you can affect their lives. I challenge you Thomas, see how many smiles you can collect for the rest of your life."

Pops still continued to teach. "How many times do you say hello to the women upstairs in the football office. Do you know if they have a family? Do you ask them about their plans for the weekend? How was their day? Do they drink coffee in the morning? What about the GAs (graduate assistants) do you speak to them? Or do you treat them like servants? If Coach Carroll were in the office, would you speak to him? Would you ask him questions?"

"Well, yeah. Of course I would."

"Why would you do that?"

I shrugged.

"Because he has something to give you. He has the control to play you more or less, of course you would speak to him. Well, Thomas, these other people matter too. They matter because they are people and regardless of whether they can help your or not, they might one day be in the position to help you. They will always remember you used to speak to them when they had nothing, of course they will help you when they have everything. Treat the janitor like the CEO and the CEO like the janitor. Because everyone is equal and you never know who is who. If you treat everyone the same, then you never have to worry about trying to figure out who's who."

Legacy Goes Beyond Your Stats

Look at where you are right now, athletically. As athletes, we uphold the standards the people who came before us have set. I went to USC and learned exactly what it meant to be a USC Trojan. I had to ask myself, "Thomas, are you doing everything you can to continue that legacy?"

I assumed I was.

On the flip side, I consider the academic legacy of attending USC. There were no college graduates in my family before I went to USC. After graduating from USC, I became determined to be sure the legacy of college graduates would become normal in my family.

That is my legacy.

Some of you, perhaps, have a long line of family members who have gone to college. Look at how you're upholding that legacy by attending college yourself. How does it feel to know you are continuing the legacy?

Forget the plays you make and the final scores. People will remember forever how you treated them. There are people who reach out to me, "Hey, we went to school together." They often comment on how I never treated them as though I was better than they were. This is after ten years have passed and they still remember how I made them feel. My legacy as a player was good. My legacy as a person means much more.

Giving Back to Your Community

Think back to when you were in elementary school and you saw a high school athlete, college athlete, or even a professional athlete. You may have said, "One day, that is going to be me." Well, that one day is here, and you are a college athlete. You have worked hard and you are now in a position to represent your university by playing at such a high level.

Now, it's your chance to be that inspiration you experienced when you were younger. The torch has been passed. You are responsible for showing the next generation they too can live out their dreams exactly as you did. Your surrounding community is an extension of your college or university. For all student athletes, we have a platform to ignite and inspire our surrounding neighborhoods. We are the hope for those communities.

As a requirement for one of my sociology classes, I took part in the Joint Educational Program (JEP) a program founded in 1972 that offers USC students an opportunity to give back to the community surrounding USC. I participated in JEP for my entire college career and it gave me a completely new perspective.

During my upbringing, I felt I struggled all my life being a biracial child growing up without my dad in my life. There were times when we didn't have a lot and I had to wear last year's fashion in shoes and sporting gear because we couldn't afford the latest and the greatest. Getting a scholarship to USC was a dream come true for me. Without my scholarship, I would not have been able to get a free education. That first semester with JEP, I got paired with a middle school in the area not more than five miles from the USC campus. It was there I learned my status as a USC football player meant more than I could have ever imagined.

I had no expectations when I first joined JEP. All I knew was my grade in class depended on my participation. I signed up for weekly visits and knew I would be there for an hour to mentor, or help the students with their homework.

During one of my first visits, the teacher told me they have thirty students in the class. When I looked around, I saw half of them were missing. Where were they?

This was the first moment I realized real struggles our youth face. Four of five of them couldn't come to school on Tuesdays because that's the day drug dealers hung out at the bus stop, or gangs hung around outside their home so they didn't feel safe walking to the bus stop. Some had to stay home and care for their younger siblings because their mom worked three jobs and couldn't afford daycare. Some kids slept in the classroom because it was the only safe place to sleep because their parents strung themselves out on drugs and kept the kids up all night. I also learned this school provided snacks for the students in the morning because some of the students didn't have meals at home.

One day I remember asking the teacher about the student's study habits at home.

The teacher explained to me the school only had one set of books for each subject. As a result, the students could not take the books home to study.

"Why don't they look up their science project at home on the computer?" I asked.

"They don't have computers at home and the school only has six for the entire school," the teacher replied.

I developed a great deal of compassion and empathy for the students I worked with. They didn't grow up like I did. For the first time in my life, I understood, for as bad as I thought my life had been growing up in a nontraditional household, my mom wasn't hooked on drugs. I didn't have to worry about my route to school because of gang shootings. I didn't have to take a bus twenty-five miles because it was the only safe school I could go to.

My passion for serving and inspiring people came from these experiences. I grew up thinking I had a tough life and my JEP experience illustrated there are plenty of people who have it a lot worse.

I also learned how powerful my status as a student athlete was.

I'd walk into those classrooms and the kids would say, "You're on the football team?" They were thrilled when we would come to their school. I wasn't even getting a bunch of playing time. I was not the star of the team, yet they looked at me as if I were. To have a USC football player in their classroom was an experience they wouldn't forget when their reality was to survive some of the harshest circumstances imaginable. I discovered many students did not have a father present at home. The presence my teammates and I provided gave them a different goal to aspire to instead of the everyday life they were used to seeing.

I saw my level of influence, and it humbled me.

I got more from those students than I was able to give to them. They gave me a perspective about how difficult it was in their neighborhoods. It stopped me from complaining that I wasn't the starter on the number one football team in the country. If that was my biggest complaint, I had a great life.

The more you give to your community, the more your community gives back to you. When we make a difference in our community, we get more fans to support us. Another great thing about community service is it can go on your resume, which is something we'll talk about in the last section of the book.

How do you give back to your community? In what ways do you feel rewarded that have nothing to do with scores and your position on the team?

Questions:

Remember the first time you met an athlete you looked up to? What did they do that made you remember them?

_____

_____

_____

Your Legacy: As a celebrity to young kids, you have the power to inspire them. How can you use your status as an athlete to encourage them to follow their dreams?

_____

_____

_____

_____

_____

What programs or events do you participate in to inspire the community that surrounds your school?

_____

_____

_____

_____

_____

What are you known for outside the lines and off the court?

_____

_____

_____

_____

_____

Outside of sports, what do you want your legacy to be?

_____

_____

_____

_____

_____

Your legacy is not the number of points you score. Your legacy is a reflection of the impact you have on others.

CHAPTER 12

Networking – Part I

Meet Keith Rivers

My time at USC provided me with opportunities far beyond simply playing the game of football. While, at first I saw new recruits coming into USC as a threat to my position on the team, I soon realized I was actually meeting some of the next great names in football and some people who would become friends for a lifetime.

One such recruit was Keith Rivers.

A five star recruit, Keith played football at Lake Mary High School in Florida and came to USC for a visit in December of my freshman year. I will admit my first thought was, *Whoa! This guy is built like a brick wall!*

I was one of Keith's hosts on his recruiting trip and my job was to show Keith around. I realized he was right where I was a year ago, stepping onto the USC campus for the first time, excited about becoming a USC Trojan. I took hosting Keith seriously because I knew we needed players like him if we wanted to keep winning at USC. I not only made impression on my future teammate, I also made a lifetime friend.

Keith donned the USC #55 jersey. He was All-Conference, All-American, and the rest is history.

The signs were all there by his sophomore year that Keith was headed to the NFL and sure enough, he was selected ninth overall by the Cincinnati Bengals and later playing for the New York Giants and the Buffalo Bills. He played until his retirement in 2015.

When I knew I wanted to include information about networking in my book, I immediately thought of Keith Rivers. I will share my insight into networking in the next chapter. For now, I want you to hear how Keith networks, because he's a natural and one of the best at networking.

Keith is a guy who "gets it."

Our experiences at USC were similar, but as I observed Keith through our years as teammates, I could see he maximized his college experience. He took advantage of every opportunity that came his way. While I was writing this book, I caught up with Keith and asked if he'd be willing to share his perspective with you. Here's what he had to say:

I came to USC from a small high school in Lake Mary, Florida. Football in high school was easy for me. College ball was different, and I faced adversity I had never experienced before. I felt I didn't play much my freshman year, which felt like a bit of a rocky start. It did give me the opportunity to do other things at USC.

We all learn no matter how good you are at something, there are people out there who are better. I used to be the best player on the field in high school. In college, I was no longer the best. Like a lot of kids, I had dreams about playing NFL, but playing football at USC made me realize there might be other things in life.

Football became a means to an end.

I set myself apart from football by focusing on myself as a person first and as an athlete second. Realizing that, I used the school for what USC is known for.

Networking opportunities

I learned USC has one of the top alumni bases in the country.

I would be a fool to go through USC and not network and build friend-ships with people outside of football.

When I was a kid, my dad used to take me around to different neigh-borhoods and asked me, "Where do you want to live when you grow up? Who you hang around with will determine where you end up in the fu-ture."

At USC, I met people whose parents not only had a good job, but they owned companies. Whoever thought I'd meet a kid whose parents own the Milky Way company? That changed my perception of the world.

We are only limited by what we don't do.

When I was in seventh grade, I got expelled from school for acting out. I could have gone a couple directions at that point, but my dad helped me see hanging around with the wrong people would limit my future.

I tried a different approach and hung around with kids who did NOT get into trouble.

At USC, I diversified the people I hung out with, because I knew once I was done with football, every other football player would be in the same place.

How were they going to help me succeed in life if we were all in the same place?

I quickly learned if you're the smartest person in the group, you're in the wrong crowd. You need to hang out with people who are smarter than you are, who know things you don't know, and then pick their brains.

Because I left my home state to go to USC, I had a lot of opportunities to meet all kinds of people because I wasn't able to go home for the weekends the way a lot of kids did. Instead, the kids who went home for the weekend invited me to go with them and I met all kinds of people. This really opened my eyes to the world. I learned to network in front of the parents of my classmates.

I didn't want to be seen as a knucklehead athlete.

I wanted to be seen as a sharp and successful person.

Many of those families had wealth like I had never seen before. They were definitely on to something I didn't know about. I knew being good at football gave me the chance to get drafted into the NFL and make some money. THESE were the people who might be able to get me a job once I was done with football. With USC having the alumni base it does, these were the people who would be giving out jobs in the future, not my football homies. These kids were the ones excelling in school and their parents excelled in business. During my senior year at USC, I met a woman from Georgetown who introduced me to her friend. His family OWNS the Dodgers. That's what networking is all about, opening up your world and seeing who you CAN meet.

One thing I did that set me on a different networking track was I chose a college major that wasn't typical for an athlete. I chose Public Policy Development. In that way, I immediately had a different crowd of classmates who did not play football. This also helped me to see my time playing football as a business. The most successful people in the world aren't afraid to start a business, and they also know you sometimes have to close a business. In my mind, once I stopped playing football at USC, I'd closed my college football business and proceeded to open up my next business, and that was my NFL football business.

My first year in the NFL was a revelation.

I broke my jaw in two places and had to have surgery to repair it. Hanging out with non-football friends helped me to see I had choices. I mean, these guys don't break their jaws and have surgery, and they have a lot more money than I do. The wheels continued to turn in my mind and I continued to build my network. I wanted to spend time with people who have perspective and knowledge in an arena I don't have.

Any advice I have is exactly this:

- *Spend time with the people who embody the life you want to lead.*

- *Learn to network and then develop relationships with people who are smarter than you are.*

- *Find people who are good at something and sit down with them and pick their brain.*

- *Study the greats. I know everyone says this but it's true. I didn't understand it until I looked back at my football career. No one expects you to have all the information, whether it is football or business. In football, we studied taped film of upcoming opponents, learning what they do and how to manage them in the game. I also studied film to get better at what I did. The same applies to business. Study what other successful people have done.*

I read constantly now, trying to bottle everything I learn as I prepare for my next business.

Keith Rivers is, in my opinion, one of the greats. Throughout his entire career at USC, he networked like a natural. He saw his opportunities at USC and took advantage of every one of them. The way I see it, Keith never left anything on the table. That's exactly what a successful business owner does, takes advantage of every available opportunity.

Take a few moments to consider opportunities you have right now that you might not be using. Remember, you're a person first, an athlete second.

What can you do to develop your network outside your chosen sport?

Questions:

How many close friends would you say you have outside of athletics? List them:

How often do you spend time with people outside of athletics?

_____

_____

_____

_____

_____

What can you learn from your friends who are not athletes?

_____

_____

_____

_____

What do your friends, who are not athletes, admire about you?

_____

_____

_____

_____

What do you admire about your friends who are not athletes?

_____

_____

_____

_____

_____

Your network will determine your net worth.

CHAPTER 13

Networking – Part II

Every student at your school is there to figure out what career path they want for the next twenty years. Many of them will go on to do wonderful things after their college graduation, in every field of work imaginable. Many of them will go on to become top executives or CEOs of a company.

But today, they are your classmates and your fans come game day.

If you learn to make friends with them while you are both attending college, your chances of them remaining friends when they become owners of corporations are good. Then your job options increase.

Think about this; the next game you play in, look into the stand and notice how many students are in attendance. Your classmates are yelling and screaming for your team to win. Deep down inside, they may want to be you. Most of them wish they could *know* you. If that is what they want, let them.

One of the greatest skills anyone can learn is networking. You heard from Keith Rivers in the previous chapter about how he took advantage of every opportunity during his time at USC to meet people outside his arena of football.

At first, I didn't quite understand the benefit to that. Shouldn't we spend time building relationships with our teammates? Of course, we should . . . at the risk of becoming one-dimensional. It is only when we connect with people in the world do we learn things we don't know.

Making Friends With Non-Athletes

Look around you on campus. There are thousands of people you don't know and may not even meet. Who should you meet, and how? As Keith mentioned in the previous chapter, look for students who are succeeding. Maybe start with a student in one of your classes. They might be able to help you improve your grade by getting involved in one of their study groups. This is where your position as a student athlete can work to your advantage because you are an expert in something they aren't.

One thing about sports, it's a universal topic.

I recently attended a seminar on entrepreneurship, and of the thirty people from eight countries there, three of us had been professional athletes. Everyone wanted to talk to us, because we had knowledge they didn't. It works the same way in college. Don't be afraid to leverage your expertise to expand your network.

Another tip I learned from watching Keith was I tried to eat lunch with non-athletes a few times a week. Most of us ate our meals at the Galen Center, a place packed with athletes. When I looked closer, there were a lot of people who worked on the administration side of athletics. I would find people I didn't know and sit down next to them. At first, it felt awkward.

But soon I learned the easiest way to communicate with new people.

What is everyone's favorite topic or theme?

Themselves, right?

People love talking about themselves. So I learned how to ask people about THEM. I asked them questions about their job, where they were from, if they had a family, or what they liked to do as a hobby.

The first few times it felt awkward.

The more I talked to people about themselves, the easier it got.

I tried to remember something special and specific about them. That way, the next time we met, I would be able to bring that up in our conversation. Remembering something about them made that person feel special. Just as I had felt when Coach Carroll would bring up something he and I talked about in a previous conversation. I wanted to do the same for the new people I met.

In order for us to meet new people and grow our network, we must be willing to get out of our comfort zone and get a different perspective of the world.

Make Fans Feel Like Friends

Every game you play in, at home or away, there are tens of thousands of fans who stop what they're doing that day to come to the game. Every single person sitting in the stands wishes they could be you for the moment. They cheer your name, wave banners, and wear your jersey all because you excite their Saturday afternoons or whenever game day is for you. Show them you are human and you are friendly by taking a few moments to sign autographs, take photos, and connect with them. You might only have ten seconds with people but you can make that ten seconds feel a lot longer for whomever you speak with. Whether you are on campus, on the field, or in the community, take time to acknowledge them. You never know who that fan is.

You will be remembered by the plays you made but more importantly, you will be remembered by the impact you make individually to the fans when you were not between the lines. If you play in front of 50,000 people every game, that means you have 50,000 opportunities to turn fans into friends.

Don't see only faces in the stands.

See opportunities in the stands.

This goes for adults, children and students on campus. Remember, you're doing something all your fans wish they could do. The iron is hottest while you are playing. Your flame decreases the moment you are no longer a current student athletes.

One day I left the stadium and noticed a woman and her little girl. They appeared to be waiting for me. I love meeting fans, so I put a big smile on my face and approached them. The girl's face lit up as she asked if I would mind if she took my photo. Of course not. When they took as many pictures they wanted, I asked if I could take a picture in order to remember them

As they began to leave, the girl's mother turned around and said, "Thank you. I wasn't sure if you'd pay any attention to my daughter. I really appreciate it."

I must have looked as surprised as I felt.

"I mean, you're the Hitman on the field. You're like a monster out there. I wasn't sure if you'd take time to speak with us."

That's when it hit me, my reputation on the field might be the way people perceive me off the field. After that experience, I made it a huge point to start talking and chatting with fans, knowing that a single experience could have lasting effects.

Remember, you never know who that fan is. They are looking up to you now as a player but when you stop playing and you have made them feel like your friends, they will return the favor and that can look like a job, an opportunity. By making your fans feel like friends, you are showing people another side of you, that you're not just an athlete.

By doing this, you are adding to your network.

What To Do With Those Business Cards

Successful athletes aren't looking only for their edge in sports; they also look for a competitive edge in life.

One of my mentors saw me talking to a gentleman outside the locker room one day after practice and he asked me who I was talking to. I told him who the guy was, I remembered his name, but I had no idea what made him so special. My mentor told me a little about the gentleman, that he was a very successful real estate mogul who owned a good part of the city.

He suggested I reach out immediately.

"Why?" I asked. I didn't need anything from him.

That day, my mentor gave me a huge nugget I want to give to you, so you can use it for the rest of your life. He said, "You contact him to tell him you enjoyed meeting him. That way you start to develop communication with him." My mentor went on to tell me that he was a very important businessman, and probably meets dozens of people every single day. "But if you contact him now, letting him know it was a pleasure meeting him, you'll set yourself apart from the crowd because he'll remember meeting you."

After that day, I noticed a bunch of my teammates would take the same business cards and pocket them, yet most of them never called the name on the card, or sent an email. I made it a habit to reach out to at least one person I had met each week. I didn't want anything from these people; I wanted to stay fresh in their minds.

This reminded me of another life lesson I learned in sports. Do what others won't, when others won't, in order to set yourself apart. This is why I began to make it a habit of reaching out to say hello to people, usually by email, after they gave me their business cards.

Because I'd already been practicing using people's names and remembering something personal about them, I began to do that with my business card contacts as well. I'd put Thomas Williams: USC football player in the subject line of an email. Then I would recap what we talked about when we had met. If I remembered he was going out of town for a weekend in Mexico with his wife, I made sure to mention I hoped they had a great time.

I found out in a big hurry I separated myself from the others by doing this. The next time I met that individual in person, I had something to follow up with, "How was that trip to Mexico with your wife?"

People are often amazed when you take the time to remember something specific about them. It's one of the most powerful tools I've learned for networking.

Being genuine is the key. People must feel like you're genuinely interested.

Don't pretend to be something you're not. However, learning to network is not a natural ability. It is a skill that can be developed and enhanced each and every time you do it.

Close One Business, Open Another

No matter how you look at it, playing sports is a business.

And that business, even in college, takes your time, talent, and treasure. Keith Rivers helped me to see even playing in football in college is like running a business; you give it your all.

Not all businesses last forever. There are plenty of start-up businesses that run a few years and then either fails or is sold to someone who can do it better. Robert Kiyosaki, of *Rich Dad, Poor Dad* talks about the number of businesses he started and how many of them ended prematurely. The reason he became wealthy was because he constantly prepared for the next business.

You can't prepare for your next business without networking.

To give you an overview of businesses started by college students, check out the following list of some of today's most valuable startups:

- 1923 Britton Hadden and Henry Luce from Yale founded Time Magazine, the first weekly news magazine in the US, and today is the most widely circulated after People Magazine.

- 1981 Bill Gates and Paul Allen licensed MS-DOS to IBM, becoming co-founders of <u>Microsoft</u>. (Bill attended Harvard for only a year, then left to work on his enterprise.)
- 1984 Michael Dell, undergrad of Texas University, created <u>Dell</u>, the number one shipper of PC monitors in the world.
- 1995 Jerry Yang and David Filo, Stanford graduate students founded <u>Yahoo</u>.
- 1998 Larry Page and Sergey Brin also graduates of Stanford, founded <u>Google</u>. They struggled to balance their start-up and their schoolwork, but managed to keep both going.
- 2004 Mark Zuckerberg and fellow students at Harvard dreamed up <u>Facebook</u>, the social media giant.
- 2007 Drew Houston and Arash Ferdowski, both from MIT developed <u>Dropbox</u> because they had trouble sending big files over the internet. Over 200 million people use their service, making them the leader in file sharing on the internet.
- 2008 Karina Pikhart, undergraduate student at MIT and Robert Liebert developed <u>6 Dot</u>, a technology that easily make braille labels for the visually impaired. They got their company off the ground after a successful Kickstarter campaign.
- 2011 Stanford University students Evan Spiegel and Robert Murphy developed <u>Snapchat</u>, the message that lasts only seconds. They were recently offered over four billion dollars for their creation.

Most students encounter challenges. Student athletes are no different. The key is to believe in your vision and not give up. Every single entrepreneur in the list above struggled to balance school and working on his or her business. As a student athlete, you understand the difficulties of maintaining your athletic development while working toward your degree. No one works in a bubble, and by networking with people from many walks of life, you may be surprised at who you may bump into ten years down the road when you say, "Hey, didn't we go to school together?"

Your Networks

It was time to starting thinking about internships for my junior year. For three years, I had seen Nike reps coming in and out of the equipment room. These guys were dressed in Nike jumpsuits and seemed as though they had a really good life. I found out some of these reps made six figures and spent most of their time traveling to universities in their region.

I asked Pops what a Nike rep does and he explained to me.

It seemed to me they had a great job, talking all day long about Nike. What better person to talk about Nike, than myself, someone who trained in Nike, played in Nike, and loved Nike. Sounded like a no brainer.

I wanted to get more information about the job description of a Nike rep and decided to ask Ken Norton what he thought about the idea.

He loved it.

Even better, he had the perfect person for me to meet, Kirk Reynolds. Kirk was Director of Public Relations for the 49ers when Coach Norton played for them. Ken told me to reach out to Kirk and find out if he had any connections in the Nike world.

Kirk knew an executive for Nike and gave me his contact information. That executive was Rodney Knox. I sent Rodney an email and we scheduled a time to talk on the phone.

After our call, Rodney and I never talked again on the phone. I would send him emails periodically if only to say hello. He would respond twenty-four to forty-eight hours later. I learned Rodney was impressed with my eagerness to explore my opportunities beyond the field.

Even more important than what he was impressed with, I learned about my leverage as a current student athlete on a football team, which his company sponsored. I knew Rodney was a very busy man and the chances of him forgetting about me were high. I did not want Rodney to forget about me, so I decided to remain in contact. Since I wanted a job at Nike after graduation, I felt like my best chance of getting that job was to go through Rodney. If I could build some sort of relationship with an executive at Nike, I felt like I had better chances of getting a job.

I also learned about the six degrees of separation. I didn't know Rodney at all. How did I get to him? I knew Ken, who knew Kirk, who knew Rodney. It was all because I decided to tap into my network and by doing that, I was able to connect with people I wanted to reach.

As student athletes, it can be hard to attend networking events or have meetings with people. We can network within our athletic facilities if we take full advantage of the opportunities standing before us.

Questions:

Aside from your coaches and academic support staff, who else inside of the athletic department can you develop relationships with?

_____

_____

_____

_____

_____

When you meet someone for the first time, what are 2 things you want them to remember about you?

1.

_____

_____

2.

_____

_____

Your fans see you one way on the court or on the field, how can you show them you are more than an athlete?

_____

_____

_____

_____

_____

There is an old saying, "It's not WHAT you know, but WHO you know."
Taking that a step further, it's not even about who you know.
It's about WHO KNOWS YOU!

CHAPTER 14

Relationships

We've spent a fair amount of time talking about networking and how to meet people outside our athletic bubble. Most of the new connections we make end up in a business card file because we know we should keep contact information.

We have made the connection, now what?

What do we do after we have met someone?

The next step is the development of a relationship.

Relationships are deeper than merely exchanging business cards or signing an autograph. I was well on my way to relationship development by learning a person's name and maybe something about their life or their family. I practiced it all the time.

Why?

Because I began to see the effects.

When Coach Carroll walked through the halls of USC, he would greet every person he met by name. People left his presence smiling. When he knew my name, and I wasn't even a starter, that left me with a huge grin on my face. When some of the legends of USC came to visit campus, whether for practice or for games, they were near the team and I will never forget the first time Marcus Allen called me by name. That made me feel larger than life. Wow! Marcus Allen knows who I am?

Start With People You See Every Day

After Pops gave me the talk on treating everyone with respect and compassion, I made sure I followed his advice, particularly with people I interacted with on a regular basis.

Take the equipment room staff, for example. They were there to pass out jerseys, cleats, practice pads, you name it. Players constantly went into that room with demands, and not all of them had the advantage of having had a talk with Pops the way I had. Whenever I went into the equipment room, I always made a point of greeting the guys working there by name. I asked about their lives outside of USC football. We joked about what we would do for an upcoming weekend. They got to know me, I got to know them. When I went into the equipment room, they greeted me with a smile. Any time I asked for anything, they said, "Sure, Thomas. For you, no problem."

Developing rapport with people didn't stop at the equipment room. It was useful everywhere. During the season, we would watch film of opposing teams in meetings. I didn't have the same system to view the film at home, which meant I couldn't watch the game film on the opponents as I did at school. One day, I decided to see if someone in the video department could help me. I hadn't done much about developing a relationship with the guys in that department beyond getting to know their names and a little bit of personal information; I tentatively knocked on the door and went in. I really wasn't sure how it worked. I just knew I needed to watch the film.

I started with small talk as I had learned to do. "How's your day, Eric? Good, how's the family? What did you have for lunch?" Anything at all to get the guy talking was my goal. Then I took my chance. I asked him if he wouldn't mind making me a few DVDs of our opponents. Without hesitation, he said, "Sure." He asked what games I would like to take home.

That was easier than I ever expected. I said, "You don't mind?"

"Absolutely not. Every time I see you, you're always asking about me and my family. You didn't show up and demand stuff. For you, I don't have a problem giving you something you ask for. There are other people who come in here and demand things at the last minute, expect us to stop doing what we're doing, just because they walked in here. For people like that, we don't like doing things for them. For people like you, it's not a problem. The DVDs will be in your locker tomorrow morning."

And sure enough, they were. From that moment on, I had no problem getting DVDs of our opponents. In fact, after asking a few weeks in a row, the DVDs started showing up in my locker without me even asking.

You can bet I went to the video department to thank the guys for going out of their way for me.

First Impressions

Early on when I first met people, I felt shy, insecure, and was soft spoken. I actually felt unequal to individuals who were not athletes. I used to speak softly, and give a soft handshake or sometimes no handshake at all. I know, I'm almost embarrassed to admit this, but it's the truth, and I want everyone out there to know if you've experienced this, you're not alone. It wasn't until a teammate of mine showed me how to instantly connect with people, where I understood how easy it is to develop a relationship.

We had played against Notre Dame and my grandmother attended the game with my mom and other family members. We had won the game 38 to 0. After we showered and changed, we walked up the tunnel where we met our families. Mom was there, her boyfriend, and my grandmother. I hugged them all enthusiastically.

Then one of my teammates, Taylor, happened to walk by. I introduced him to my family and he started speaking with my grandmother.

We chatted maybe ten or fifteen minutes, and then Taylor said goodbye and we started walking toward the bus.

Grandmother turned to me, "Who was that?"

"Taylor, a safety from the state of Washington. Why do you ask?"

Her answer floored me. "Thomas, that young man was raised right. The entire time we were talking, he paid attention to me. He looked me in the eyes the whole time. He made me feel as though I was the only person in the world and made me feel what I had to say was important to him. He made me believe this was the most important moment to him."

I probably nodded my head, thinking I played with this guy every single day and I never noticed that about him.

Then Grandmother pinned me to the floor with her next question, "Thomas, do you do that when you meet people? Do you look them in the eyes and pay attention to their words?"

I have to admit to numerous times when I didn't think what other people had to say was of any importance to me.

We were strangers.

But Grandmother's wisdom came through.

"Thomas, when you make people feel like they are the only person in the world, they open up to you and feel comfortable with you. You have the ability to open them up to you by making eye contact and asking questions about what they are talking about rather than thinking about what you're going to say next."

I never forgot that event.

Not that Grandmother ever let me.

Every time I spoke with her after that, she made sure to ask about Taylor, even though they had only spoken for a few minutes. I've learned since then that in any given conversation is an opportunity we have to learn a great deal about the other person. The way you can learn so much about other people is when you allow them to feel comfortable enough to open up to you.

Taylor never forged a relationship with my grandmother, but if he'd wanted to, he had already built a great foundation.

Connecting with People

We have all heard someone say, "They only call me when they want something. They never stop by just to see how I'm doing."

How can we avoid being labeled as that type of person? By stopping by, calling, or sending an email just because. Call to say, "Hey, I haven't seen you in a while. What's new?" Send an email with a message in the subject line, "Hey, checking in. Let's have coffee sometime." Stop by and ask folks how their day is going. If you're heading past a vending machine, say, "Can I get you something?" Most of the time they will turn you down. On the other hand, when you come around, not when you need something or have a demand, people are more likely to smile when they see you coming.

Take Care of the People Who Take Care Of You

During my sophomore year I was walking up to the linebacker meeting room and Ms. Joyce, one of the assistants in the office, said, "Thomas, would you like some candy?"

I said, "Yes, please!" and grabbed a few from the bowl of candy on her desk. Every time I would head to a football meeting, I would grab a few. The following day, the jar was filled up again, and I would grab a few more. It was routine, for not only me, but my teammates as well.

Every single day that jar was filled to the top.

I never thought much about it until one day she stopped me and said, "Thomas, I want to thank you for your card. I really appreciated it."

I mumbled something and went on. I had no idea what she was talking about. I found out later one of the senior linebackers had written her a note saying, "We appreciate the candy you have for us every day and want to help buy the next bag. He signed the names of all the linebackers of the team and popped in a twenty-dollar bill. That twenty wasn't nearly enough for all the candy we had been eating over the weeks, but the look on her face was priceless because the card and the money showed her how much we appreciated what she did for us every single day.

It was a great lesson on relationships and taking care of people who take care of you. She didn't have to provide the candy. We didn't have to get a card or pay her for it. But she did. And my teammate did, making the whole linebacker squad looked like gentlemen.

I learned a lot from that experience. I learned you take care of the people who are taking care of you.

Common Ground

When meeting someone new, always try to find common ground. Having common ground is the easiest and fastest way to connect with someone, especially when you meet for the first time. I don't have kids, but I played sports all the way through school. If someone I meet has kids, I try to find out what activities or sports their kids play. Over the years, I have found the most important thing to most adults who have kids is their kids. Once you get people to start talking about their kids, they light up like a Christmas tree. At that point, they have opened up and are much less guarded.

It's similar to watching film on your next opponent so many times that you know for certain when they are running a specific play. Once you have identified the play and you know it is coming, you can stop it from happening because you are tuned in with your opponent. When meeting people outside the athletic bubble, you might seem to be an opponent to them. Actually, they have the potential to be a teammate.

They don't know it yet.

Becoming MORE Than An Athlete

While you're in school, you have an identity as an athlete. There was nothing I loved more than the attention I received on the football field. But there are going to be times when you want to be seen as *more* than an athlete. Unfortunately, athletes suffer from a stigma of being not especially intelligent, and I definitely wanted to be seen as something more than a jock.

I once watched Ricky Williams interviewed on television and I'll never forget his statement, "I'm not a football player. I'm a person who plays football."

When I heard that, I knew he was on to something.

While football defined a big portion of my life, it wasn't *all* of my life.

I always hated it when working on group projects for a class and I'd come up with an idea everyone liked. They always managed to put me down by saying, "You're pretty smart for a football player." The same thing even happened when I was doing my internships, especially when I first started.

Once they found out I was on the football team, they instantly pegged me as someone who wasn't smart.

They would pepper me with questions, the most common one being, "What are you going to do if you don't make it to the NFL?" I'd been asked that so many times I had a generic answer for them that made me sound pretty smart and ambitious. Then they managed to cut me down again by saying, "For an athlete you're really articulate and ambitious." That really drove me through the roof.

Because I knew I wanted to be seen as more than just an athlete, I started telling people I play football and I have other hobbies and passions outside of football. This allowed people to see other aspects of me as a person and not just an athlete.

The same goes for you. You are more than an athlete. Identify interests and hobbies outside of sports and begin to share those with other people so they see you are more than athlete too. In terms of building relationships, the more other people learn about you, the less they will identify you as merely an athlete.

As you can see, relationship building is important for many reasons.

Questions:

Who are 3 people you would like to meet, who can help you professionally:

1.

2.

3.

Write the names of 3 people who you see often, who do so much for you and they go unannounced or unnoticed:

1.

_____

2.

_____

3.

_____

What steps will you take to expand your networking skills into developing relationships?

_____

_____

_____

_____

_____

Six things to focus on when first meeting someone:

- *Have a firm handshake.*
- *Make eye contact.*
- *Remember a person's name.*

- *Listen to them as if what they have to say is the only thing that matters.*
- *Remember something specific from a conversation you had with that person.*
- *If given a business card or contact information: Follow up immediately. Email, phone call (24 hours from the time you met them).*

Remember, people are more likely to help you out when:

- *They like you*
- *They know that you care about them.*
- *You don't only come around when you need something*

CHAPTER 15

Leadership

Countless books speak on the topic of leadership.

I am not the guru on leadership, but I have been a part of some of the best teams that display great leadership and also a part of teams that lacked characteristics of leadership.

What I want to focus on is leadership as it applies to student athletes.

Some of our first leader choices might be our coaches or the older players on the team. How do you know when someone is a good leader?

Let's start with the definition of leadership:

- The action of leading a group of people or organization
- The state or position of being a leader

When you look at those two definitions of leadership, you probably have a picture of some of the leaders in your life. Maybe a captain who has been appointed by your coaches, maybe the point person for a group assignment, or any other person who is in charge. The truth is, just because someone is in a leadership position does not necessarily mean they are good leaders. And some people, who are not assigned the leader position, demonstrate great leadership.

Identify and Follow Good Leaders

Leaders are those around us who have a vision of their goal, take steps to achieve that goal, and manage to inspire and empower people around them to do the same.

When Ken Norton, Jr. joined the USC team as the linebacker coach, I was beyond excited. I still remember walking past Coach Carroll's office and waving a hand inside the door as I went by. Coach said, "Come on in and meet your new coach." I saw a big man in a cowboy hat turn to face me, sticking his hand out to shake mine. I couldn't believe it. The whole time I played football in Vacaville, Ken Norton, Jr. number 51 of the San Francisco 49ers was one of my favorite players. He played linebacker. I played linebacker. His dad was a boxer. My dad was a boxer. I even wore the same facemasks and use the same type of mouthpiece when I was in high school. To be shaking hands with one of my all-time football idols was exciting. For him to be my coach was a dream come true.

It was during the time I grew under his coaching when I recognized him as a true leader. He wasn't your typical coach who just yelled and screamed. He asked his players questions, figured out what made us feel good, what motivated and inspired us, and he used those things to individually coach us. We shared his vision of ourselves and became better football players as a result of his leadership style of coaching.

He coached us as people first, as players second.

I learned as much about life and dealing with people from Ken Norton, Jr. as I did about playing linebacker on the field. He was a true leader in that he inspired me to be the best version of myself both on and off the field. It was from him I learned to take full advantage of every opportunity while I played for USC, to leave nothing on the table.

Peer Leaders

Aside from leadership in the shape of a coach, several teammates taught me a great deal about both football and life without ever being told they were leaders. During my first year at USC, I went through a period where I thought I wouldn't make it as a football player for USC. I'd called my mom, almost begging to come home. I felt so overwhelmed I wanted to go home and hide.

I was looking for an easy way out.

When a rumor started that instead of practice one day, Coach Carroll was going to surprise us with a bone. Talk was going around that the team would skip practice and go downtown to attend the X-Games. The entire team seemed to totally believe we would not practice that day. Everyone went through the motions of putting on their equipment, expecting Coach to surprise us.

I was a freshman, so I didn't think anything of it.

I was happy we weren't going to have practice that day. When we got to the locker room, I geared up, but I didn't do everything I normally did. I didn't tape my wrist or ankles. I didn't even take my gloves out to practice with me. As I passed one of my teammates, Keary Colbert, an upperclassman, I noticed him taking his time to fully gear up. I remember thinking; doesn't everybody know we aren't practicing today?

Keary was going through his pre-practice routine, putting everything on, his cleats, his shoulder pads.

I asked, "Why are you putting on your pads already? Don't you know we are going to the X-Games?"

Keary looked at me and said, "I don't know what everyone else is doing, I'm getting ready for practice." I was thinking here's a senior going through his full pre-practice routine. Why is he not getting ready for the X-games like the rest of us? Out on the field, Coach Carroll blew the whistle and this is when we thought he would announce the cancellation of practice.

He said, "We are not going to the X-Games. Whatever you need to do to get your minds right, do it, because we are here to practice."

I felt way out of tune that day. I thought, if I had the same mindset that Keary did, I would have been mentally prepared for practice.

As a player, Keary was the type of leader every coach wants in their locker room. After USC, the Carolina Panthers drafted Keary in the second round. He was the type of leader who rarely said much but his actions spoke volumes in the locker room. From that moment on, external factors like the X-games rumors stopped mattering. In that moment, Keary demonstrated that having a routine is one of the best habits any successful person can have.

When similar rumors went around again, I never believed them. Keary demonstrated leadership by example.

For yourself, find out who is doing things right and follow their lead.

Are You a Leader?

Before any great leader can lead, they must first learn to follow. Leadership is a culture, a mindset. Coaches can try to lead, but if no one follows them, they become ineffective and are not leaders. In my experience as a football player, I watched as some of my teammates really listened to the coach and they would absorb what the coach is teaching, his philosophy, and then bring it into the locker room and then it would transfer to the field.

Those players were leaders.

Some of them had a C on their jersey that symbolized captain. Others did not have a C, and they were all leaders.

You may notice when a coach goes to a new pro team, they often bring a player with them; someone who knows their style of coaching and can spread the coach's message throughout the locker room.

Having that veteran player spread the word to the team solidifies the example that the coach may be the leader, but there needs to be leadership from players in order for the team to be efficient.

When I first arrived at USC, there were upperclassmen in the locker room who already knew the drill. They knew Coach Carrol's philosophy and how he ran his team. They didn't complain, they didn't try to find a shortcut to success because they believed in their coach, his vision, because he had proven to them his style produced champions.

The seniors, especially, didn't want to play their last year at any level less than championship caliber.

By watching the actions of those upperclassmen, I began to understand that sometimes people tell you what they want you to do. Real leaders show you how to do something. The best leaders do twice as much as they ask others to do. By working as hard as they can, the leaders can expect more from those of us who are new to the culture.

All leaders were once followers.

As a younger player, I observed the older players who assumed unofficial leadership roles. When they made a good decision, the team would accomplish the ultimate goal. When the leaders made a bad decision, the entire team failed right along with him.

More importantly, good leaders have to know exactly what they want their team to accomplish.

What is the goal?

The next question is: What standards will I hold myself to and are they the same standards for everyone else?

If a leader holds his followers to higher standards than he holds for himself, failure is a likely result.

I used to watch a show called *Undercover Boss*, where the CEO or founder of the company goes undercover to do several different jobs in his business to see if they can figure out ways to improve their business and to see what went on day in and day out at various locations.

I love this example of leadership because most CEOs are getting a taste of the operational side of their business and they are clueless as to how it operates. Many leaders of companies say they want growth and greater productivity, yet they don't know how to do even the smallest task their employees have to do every day.

This is a perfect example where the leader (CEO) expects more from their employees and managers than they do for themselves.

Keys to a Winning Culture: Leadership

As a leader, you have to have a solid vision for yourself and for your team. Here are a few things to keep in mind to stay in the winner's circle:

1. Know your desired outcome- Know the ultimate goal! Be specific!
2. Hold yourself to a higher standard than those following you.
3. Do twice as much as you're asking your followers to do.
4. Do the little things well and the big things take care of themselves.
5. Get people to believe in the same vision.
6. Encourage twice as much as you criticize.

Questions:

Think back to some of the great leaders you have seen. Who are some of the most effective leaders you have been around?

What makes a great leader in your eyes?

_____

_____

_____

_____

_____

Leaders:

- *Are humble enough to know they do not know everything.*
- *Are those who have been great followers.*
- *Lead from the front of pack, middle of the pack and back of the pack.*
- *Get to know the others around them on a personal level.*

In order to be a great leader you must: <u>know the way</u>, <u>show the way</u>, and <u>go the way!</u>

PART IV

LIFE BEYOND SPORTS

CHAPTER 16

Transferrable Skills

It's about time for you to see how *great* it is to be a student athlete, and how you can take what you're learning in your sport with you into the rest of your life. When I travel the country to teach my Student Athlete Player Development Program, I drive this point home. As student athletes, you have a special set of skills you've learned as an athlete, and I want you to use them to make yourselves elite wherever you show up in the world. By recognizing these skills, you will be in the top five percent for life.

These are called Transferrable Skills.

A transferrable skill for you as a student athlete is something you have learned on the field, on the court, one you can take with you into another part of your life. You're already doing it with some of your classes. Student athletes are expected to learn a lot of information in a short period of time. Your professors and instructors all count on you to retain the information being taught. You've' learned to do this when your coaches talk to you. Being attentive, a fast learner and being coachable are all transferrable skills; whether you learned these skills in a classroom setting or through your sport. These valuable skills help you in your sport and will be extremely valuable long after your time as an athlete.

In this chapter, I will help you identify some of your transferrable skills as well as show you how to use them for the rest of your life. You might not need to throw a 50-yard pass in the next part of your life, but you will take all the training that went into you being able to throw that pass into the corporate world with you.

Once a Skill, Always a Skill

That's the good news, isn't it?

Sometimes as a student athlete, I felt overwhelmed putting in twelve to fourteen hour days. I often thought non-athletic students had it easy. All they had to do was go to class and study. Student athletes have to adhere to the constant demands of their sport, put in practice hours, and still be able to compete in the classroom.

The first time someone mentioned something like working or an internship, I wanted no part of that. I didn't think it was possible to have an internship and focus on my academics and athletics. I didn't think my brain had enough room in it to learn something new. Our USC playbook resembled a four-inch thick telephone book for a major metropolitan area. As students, we lugged around a backpack full of books for classes each term or semester. That's a lot of learning we had to do. As a result, I didn't want to learn anything new.

But, I did need more money to make ends meet every month, and when I learned an internship would pay me, I figured I would go ahead and learn whatever skills I needed to get a paycheck every two weeks from my internship.

What I discovered myself and from talking with other athletes who worked during the off-season is most of the skills our sports have taught us are some of the same skills employers want their employees to have.

Transferrable Skills

As top athletes in your sport, you already have the following skill-set:

- **Tenacity**

   How many of you have ever worked with a group of students on a project and the plan was to meet for two hours at the student union? When you arrive, you discover not every single person is on time. Not every participant is even prepared. Sometimes part of the group doesn't even show up. You talk, maybe breaking the ice a bit, and suddenly your two hours are up and someone checks the time and says, "Ok, two hours are up. Time to go." You're sitting there thinking, Hey, we didn't work on the project at all.

   Any time we were practicing and had plays we needed to master we often stayed after practice and ran the play over and over again until we got it right. That's tenacity. Sitting there jawing for two hours and getting nothing done on a project is not. As an athlete, you don't stop until the job is complete. Remember this; most people go home when the time is up. As an athlete, you don't go home until the job is finished. Embody this, and there won't be a job in the world that will overwhelm you.

- **Working as a Team**

Every single athlete who has played a team sport has had at least one teammate who they didn't get along with. That doesn't mean you're a bad person, or that they are. Not every person in the world is going to get along with every other person in the world. It's part of human nature. You *do* know how to work as a team.

As a student, again in a group project situation, you might have one or more participants in your project you don't click with. Your grade on the project depends on how well you work together as a team. On the field, if your coach sees you slighting another team member, you're going to hear about it. Even the rest of your team will get after you, because you're only strong and effective when you all work toward getting a victory.

This skill transfers to your academic life and you can bet it will transfer to life after sports. All too often, businesses suffer because they don't have a team mentality, and they can't seem to get past the idea that because they don't like someone they work with, they won't do as good a job on their project. Being a team player teaches you to put personal feelings aside and get the job done. One day your employer may ask you, "Can you show/teach how my people can be better team players? Do you understand how that dynamic works?" Of course you do, because you have been a teammate most of your life.

- ## Learning OUTSIDE the Classroom

For some students, if it wasn't taught in class or it's not in the textbook, then they don't feel they need to know it. As an athlete, if you don't know how to do something, you know how important it is to ask or you're not going to get it right in the game. Book learning, classroom learning is only the beginning. Just as your playbook is only the beginning. How you put it to use is the practical application of what you learned and you continue to learn, refine, and discover new concepts. As an athlete, you *know* how to find the answer to your problem or question, you don't stop when you can't find it in the playbook.

PROFESSIONALS do it until they get it right.

CHAMPIONS do it until they can't get it wrong.

You, my friend, are a champion.

- ## Second Wind

This is otherwise viewed as going the extra mile. During my first year at USC I thought I was working pretty hard, but as I've already admitted, I felt plenty intimidated by the great athletes around me. Initially, I was content to just sit back and watch and do only as much as the coaches asked, never doing any more than I needed, but I wasn't exceling.

After watching my roommate, Reggie, recover from an injury, chafing at the bit to get back to training, I realized unless I pushed myself to the limit, I would not know what my second wind felt like. Could you imagine if a perfect pass wasn't caught because the receiver stopped running because he was tired? You train for that second wind because you never know when you need it. I've talked to plenty of people who mention a really big deadline at work and how some of them and their teams work a lot of overtime, even weekends to meet their goal, while other people say they put their forty hours in and they will finish the job next week. If you had to guess which business is more successful, which business would you say?

- **Laser Focus**

Whether it is practice or the game, as athletes, you're constantly thinking, "Do my job, make the play, win the game." There is nothing else that matters. Your only focus is your assignment for the moment. That is not something everyone in this world can do. Every top athlete has the capability of being laser-focused while playing. When you harness this skill and use it for your academic work or for a future employer, you will stand out as being highly intelligent and very productive. Employers love focused people, because getting the job done is the only thing that matters.

- **Time Management**

We spent a whole chapter on time management because it is such a vital skill for a student, especially a student athlete. Using your skills in this area won't stop after your playing career because for the rest of your life you will be bargaining with our most precious commodity . . . TIME. When I first arrived at USC, I thought my future there was indefinite, there *was* no deadline. By the end of my second year, I suddenly realized I was on the clock, and it kept ticking whether I paid attention to it or not. Time management is a life skill. Those who are especially good at it are seen as efficient and effective people. Talk about a transferrable skill. Any employer will appreciate how you juggled all your practices, classes, and internships. Most college students focus on school alone. You have mastered how to excel in your sport as well as competing in the classroom.

- **Studying**

You have been studying the playbook since the day you arrived on campus. As Keith Rivers mentioned earlier in the book, studying the greats is something successful people do, whether you're studying film of the great athletes in your sport, or you're reading books about people who have already done what you want to do and you want to avoid the pitfalls they experienced. Too many times, people tell me they haven't opened a book since college. Studying is the single most important transferrable skill in the tool set. When you make studying a habit, you continually learn, expand your knowledge and awareness. Once I realized Magic Johnson was more than simply a great basketball player, I decided I needed to learn how he made the transition into being a very successful businessman. People say the moment you stop learning, is the moment you start dying. You won't be able to play sports forever, but you can develop your mind for the rest of your life.

I could go on and on with this list. My goal is to make sure you are aware of the greatness you already own. Here's a nugget. You're already doing what companies and employers need. Understand your transferrable skills, embrace them. That way, when your career is over, you can be elite forever.

Difference Between Good and Great

When you love what you're doing, you're bringing your best, your energy, your passion, your determination.

You're a top athlete for a reason. You know how to find the fire inside of you to keep going. You may have issues with a particular person, but you know exactly how to get along with that person to get the job done.

You also know exactly how to do your job. It's not enough to show up for work and then waste time. If we did that on the field, our coaches would call us out. As an athlete, you *know* if you want more playing time, you have to work for it. That is no different than wanting a promotion or more money. You want more, you do more to get it.

Let's face it, athletes aren't normal. We are almost superhuman in what we manage to accomplish in our sport. Celebrate being abnormal. Celebrate success in its many forms.

Remember this, you might have lost two games in a row, but rather than getting defeated, you know how to pull yourself and your team together to win a championship. When you take those kinds of skills with you when you leave college, or leave your athletic career, they will serve you just as well in your next adventure. Being a champion is not associated with sports. It's something that carries over into all areas of your life.

Questions:

List some skills that make you an elite athlete.

_____

_____

_____

What are some skills you need to be a good teammate?

_____

_____

_____

Your future employers are looking for a certain set of skills to take their companies to the next level. What transferrable skills do you have that will make you an asset to any job you choose when your playing career is over?

List 5 Transferrable Skills:

1.

_____

_____

2.

_____

_____

3.

_____

_____

4.

_____

_____

5.

_____

_____

When you know what you bring to the table, you become more effective in what you do!

CHAPTER 17

Mentorship

In your mind, what is a mentor? What makes them a mentor? Some of you have mentors and maybe you don't even know it. Some of you have become mentors and you don't even realize you've been given the title. The person I want to share with you is the mentor you *discover* almost completely by accident, that person who you meet and somehow you connect with them on an incredibly deep level.

Throughout my life, I've had a few mentors like this. It's not by design. They just appear. They might be right there in front of you, but if they don't have an exalted position or a title after their name, you may think they don't meet the qualifications to be a mentor.

I say this because we have mentors all around us.

I found one in the most unlikely place, the equipment room at USC. In 2004, David B. Scott had recently been hired to work in the equipment room. I didn't know it at the time, but he had recently closed his own business. He could have come to his job at USC full of bitterness and regret his life hadn't turned out the way he planned about his previous profession. He could have embraced those negative feelings and shared them with everyone he met.

But he didn't, and that speaks to what kind of man David B. Scott really is.

You've actually already met him briefly in earlier chapters. He's Pops. One day I walked into the equipment room during the summer headed into my second year because I needed some cleats to take home to train for the upcoming season. I wanted to prepare at home during our time off, so I would come into training ready to rock and roll.

One day after our last lifting session before the season was going to start, I politely made my request. Pops waved me behind the counter. Really? I can go back there? I didn't know I was allowed back there. Every other time I'd made a request, I had to wait behind the counter until an equipment manager brought out what I was looking for.

Not that day.

Pops motioned me behind the counter saying, "Come on back here. What size cleats do you wear?"

Confused, I told him I wore a size thirteen. Pops was heading straight for a stack of brand new orange Nike boxes of cleats.

"Are you sure you want to give me those?" I asked.

"You're a football player, aren't you?"

"Yes."

"And you need cleats to practice, right?"

"Yes."

"Do you want these or not?" He handed me a brand new box of cleats.

I took them, still puzzled.

"Thomas, I don't care if you're a starter or a new recruit, in my eyes you're a football player. If you need cleats, you get 'em. Every one is the same to me. No one is better than anyone else is. I treat everyone I meet with love and respect because that's the kind of man I am."

I felt a connection with Pops that day. I felt he cared about me as a person. Because of that connection, Pops became a mentor.

It was never an official position. No one introduced me to him telling me Pops was going to be my mentor for the next four years. It wasn't any kind of an official program.

And that's the beauty of finding a mentor who sees you, sees your potential, and has nothing to gain or lose by helping you out.

Pops never asked anything of me but for me to do my best. A great mentor wants the very best for you, and wants nothing from you.

I took those cleats home and every single time I put them on, I remembered Pops saying everyone he meets is an equal. No one is better than anyone else.

I wasn't used to this.

Usually people do things for others because they expect something in return. That day I felt the sincerity in Pops. His genuine heart made me feel he cared about the man I would become and not the player I was.

As student athletes, we often believe people want to meet us because we might be able to do something for them, they want something from us. That's very often true. We sometimes doubt how genuine their interest in us might be. With Pops, he wasn't trying to get anything from me. He simply treated me with respect and dignity. Every time I put those cleats on, I was reminded of the kind of man Pops was.

And that was merely the beginning.

Pops also taught me how to dress and carry myself as a business professional. If I had told Pops what I wore in my first interview, he would have been disappointed. He would have told me, showing up in a USC t-shirt and shorts was probably not the best way to make a first impression on a person in the business world who offered to pay me to intern at their company. Fortunately, at my first internship Mr. Cohen, who was a USC alumni, was delighted to provide internships to USC football players. I was lucky.

Yes, I'm going to repeat that, I got lucky that first time out. Had it been another business owner who wanted an intern who was interested in learning about business, I don't think I would have been hired for the position.

Because I hadn't met Pops yet, I was lost.

When time came for me to interview for my second internship, I told Pops about it. By then I'd been dropping by to chat with Pops on a regular basis. Pops asked me, "What are you going to wear you're your job interview?"

I looked down at my USC t-shirt and shorts, the same as I had worn to my first internship interview and said, "Probably something casual, like this."

Pops immediately began shaking his head, "Thomas, here's what you're missing. You're a football player, and for a number of years, you'll continue to be a football player. One day you're not going to be a football player. You're going to be a businessman and in order for that to happen, you need to start to act and dress like a businessman."

I'm sure I looked pretty puzzled because Pops went on to say, "I'm the USC equipment manager and I love being around all of you athletes every single day. If I had to find another job tomorrow, I'd have USC on my resume right along with all my other work experiences. Business people will hire you because of your talent on and off the football field. You have to be an asset for their company in order for them to hire you. That means even your appearance has to align with their business. You're not just a football player. When it comes to the business world, you must wear the same uniform everyone else wears. Look at it like this, the people in the corporate world are your teammates. What are they wearing in the office? You want to dress on the same level they are, because when you do that, people won't be able to look at you as an athlete. They will look at you like you are a part of their team."

Already Pops had my brain whirling. *Resume? Not play football? What was he thinking?* Because he was Pops, and I respected him I listened. Am I ever glad I did.

I said, "What should I wear to the interview?"

"A business outfit. Slacks, buttoned shirt, and a tie."

"A tie? I don't even *own* a tie."

Pops shook his head at me and smiled. "Go get a tie. Even if you have to go to Goodwill, you need to show up to your interview in a tie."

"I don't know how to tie a tie."

"No worries. Bring your tie tomorrow and I will show you how to tie it."

Not only did Pops show me how to tie it, he helped calm me down. Then he coached me the way he had been coaching me for almost a year. He reminded me when I shook hands, I was to give that person a firm handshake and look in their eyes while I did it. He encouraged me to talk to everyone in the office from the janitor to the secretary or admin assistant. "People are important and it is our responsibility to treat everyone with respect. Talk to them. Ask them how their day is going." He finished off by saying, "Thomas, make sure you take time and smile at everyone you see."

I spent four to six hours a week hanging out with Pop in his office for four years. Yes, his mentoring was that good. Most of the time we just talked. Pops would hear me out without judgment. Most of the time he never told me what to do, we talked out the issue and I eventually got to the answer on my own.

Pops always made time for student athletes, his door, his heart, and his ears were always open.

I've been gone from USC for a number of years and I still go back on campus to see Pops. He is still there talking to athletes, giving them encouragement, helping them to stand up proud and strong. Pops has the most unique ability to know every single athlete by name; all 650 of them. It didn't matter to him if you were a football player, track and field, women's diving. To him, every student was his child and lucky are those who recognized a great mentor when they met him.

In my humble opinion, the walls of USC are still standing because of Pops.

Pops was one of the first people to help me see I'm bigger than sports, I'm *more* than an athlete. I learned not everything is about me. But it *is* about finding my purpose. Every time I visit Pops, I see all the sticky notes on the wall in his office. They're personal goals of individual athletes. Those athletes use Pops as their mentor, because he'll hold them accountable to their goals. It might be getting a better grade in a specific class, or adding on weight in the weight room, or expanding their awareness and meeting people in the business world through internships and relationships. All these are life skills, and Pops mentors all the student athletes of USC better than anyone else I've ever met.

From Pops, I learned what is real in life and what is not real. It changed my views and my values. I learned to say please and thank you and to always be a gentleman. Pops could see my future and the future of many other student athletes because while he encouraged every single one of us in sports, he always reminds us, "Promise me you'll get your degree. Sports is temporary, your degree you'll have for the rest of your life."

I owe much of who I am today to Pops, one of my greatest influences.

There comes a day when you are responsible to teach what you have been taught.

From Mentee to Mentor

You'll recall when I first met Keith Rivers. During his recruiting trip, I was in charge of hosting him. My job was to show him around and do everything in my power to highlight the university. Every recruit has a host assigned to them, and if they sign with your school, you naturally become a mentor to them.

You both connect. They remind you of yourself when you first came in as a freshman. You want them to succeed and try to help them avoid some of the pitfalls you may have experienced early in your career.

Parents come on the official visits with their kids and one thing every mother said is this, "If my son comes here, take care of my baby."

I felt personally responsible for each one of the recruits I hosted. Not only did I not want to disappoint their parents, but I wanted freshmen to succeed and help us win. I also knew I wanted the team to continue the legacy set long before I ever arrived on campus. As upperclassmen, it's our responsibility to teach the younger players what we have learned.

At first, it was a lot of pressure, but I learned that by continuing to connect with their athletes when they showed up was one of the first parts of mentorship. Because I remembered what it was like when I showed up and the transition from high school to college. I wanted to do everything I could to make sure no freshman ever felt alone. I started to notice a shift in the relationships forming between myself and incoming student athletes. The more I listened without saying anything, the more trust was developed. After trust is established, the walls come down and then you can give your input.

I remember when I was eighteen years old. My entire world was spinning and I didn't have a clue what was going on. I thought I had made it and I thought I knew everything. Over the years of learning from my mistakes as well as what people had taught me, it was my obligation to share that.

Everyone who is mentored has the ability to mentor. You know you shifted from mentee to mentor when everything isn't about you. It's about the betterment of others.

Questions:

Name 3 mentors you have had. Who were they? What was their impact?

1.

_____

_____

2.

_____

_____

3.

_____

_____

How are you making lives better because of what you have learned? How are you teaching people what you have been taught?

_____

_____

_____

_____

_____

As an upperclassman, you have been through the ropes. What are you doing today to be a mentor to underclassmen who need your direction?

_____

_____

_____

_____

_____

What are key indicators that show you someone wants you to be their mentor?

_____

_____

_____

_____

_____

Mentorship is a two-way street.

First, the mentor has to be willing to share their defeats as well as their successes. Second, a mentee cannot be too proud to understand there are people who want to help them, but they must first lower their guard and be willing to listen.

CHAPTER 18

Internships

Let me ask you a question.

How comfortable would you feel if coach put one of your teammates in the game, who didn't show up to meetings, never practiced, and did not know any of the plays in the playbook? You probably would not feel comfortable playing next to that player, right? We all know there is another player on the team who has practiced, been to all of the meetings, and is more prepared than the athlete who has not. The player who has not been to practice is not reliable. They are more of a liability than an asset at that point. We would all feel more comfortable when our teammate had been to the meeting and practiced all week.

That's exactly what an internship does. The purpose of an internship is so you can get real working experience under your belt. It's that practice before the game. When you move into your next career, you will be competing against other people who went to school for a specific industry. Every summer students are working full-time internships, and many continue with part-time internships during the year.

As a student athlete, you do have more limits on your time, but you *do* have time for internships.

I know, you're busy.

You have practice. You have weights. You have tutors. You have classes.

But, during your off season or summer (depending on your sport) is when you make time for internships. When I speak with student athletes and they tell me they don't have time for an internship, all they are doing is telling me they are not utilizing all the time they are given.

Chances are, your future employment will require you to have real work experience, why not use this period of your life to get started?

Let me offer one bit of advice here, start on internships as early as possible. You can even get an internship the summer before you start college, giving you a head start on everyone else.

What You Like, What You Don't Like

A few years ago I met up with one of my former teammates. He was working in sales, cold calling people to get them to buy a product.

I asked him how he liked it and his face said it all. He absolutely hated it. Didn't he know what he was getting into before he started? That's when he told me he had never taken the time to do an internship while he was a student athlete in college. He didn't know what he liked and what he didn't like. That's one of the biggest reasons for you to make time for an internship while you're in school. A short-term internship is a good time for you to find out what you don't like. Because if you wait until you have to get a job to find these things out, it may be too late. And you find yourself stuck at a job you don't want to do, but you have to do it because you have bills to pay.

When you have several internships, it gives you a good idea about what you would like to do when you retire and what you do not want to do. Do you like to work in a cubical or a in an open office area? Do you mind wearing business attire or do you want to dress casually? Do you like to pick up the phone to cold call people or not? Do you like working in a team environment where everyone works together, or are you someone who likes to work on your own?

All of these questions can be answered when you have internship experiences.

Be Prepared For the Opportunity

Fast-forward to the end of your college career. You and another former student are sitting in the same waiting room, looking to get hired for the one job that company has.

If the person sitting in the waiting room with you has internship experience and you don't, he or she already has an advantage over you. The employer doesn't hire the other person because you're inadequate. The employer sees you as too much of a risk and does not know how long it will take for you to learn the position.

The other applicant already has work experience and can start doing the job immediately.

I Know We All Want EXTRA CASH!

As any student athlete knows, there is sometimes a lot of month left after the stipend check is spent. A way to increase cash in your bank account is to either stop spending or make more money.

Warren Buffet said it best, "Never depend on a single stream of income."

I discovered having internships gave me a little more money, and made my life at school a bit more comfortable. I knew plenty of student athletes who had to eat all their meals at the training table because they had no money left for food until their next stipend check came in.

One of my students in my Player Development program once told me he had been hired for a summer internship. He was ready to get real working experience he was going to be able to add to his resume. During the course of his internship we would touch base from time to time.

I could tell he loved the experience and he could not believe how easy it was to juggle summer workouts, summer school, and his internship.

After the internship was over, he told me he had made $5,000. After I congratulated him, I asked him what he was going to do with the money. He told me he would save it, in case he was ever running low from his stipend check.

He had found a way to get real work experience plus pocket a large chunk of money.

Not only did he make the $5,000 from his internship, he also collected his monthly stipend check for the summer school class he took.

My Internship Experiences

My first internship experience was an eye-opener for me. I heard about internships, and a big incentive was I needed the money. Some of the guys on my team had fathers who owned companies where they could get an internship. I didn't have that option. I learned about Campus Resources and they were one of my biggest assets. When I found out about the Career Center and other campus resources, someone helped me find internships and set up interviews.

Every school has some department that will help you with this. Remember, if you don't know . . . Ask!

In my case, I didn't have a car, so I couldn't drive. As a result, campus resources put me in touch with one of my teammates who had a car, and both of us got an internship with Stuart Cohen, who was a USC alumni who owned his own insurance company.

I am almost ashamed to admit this. I had never been to a job interview before, as a result, I didn't know what to wear or even how to act. Fortunately for me, Mr. Cohen was thrilled to have a couple of USC football players at his office. He didn't mind we showed up in t-shirts, shorts, and sneakers. We were supposed to file papers, answer phone calls, and draft emails. Between doing various jobs in the office, we talked about sports with Stuart and other employees in the office. It was a fun summer for me. I'm glad it was not my only internship experience, because I was incredibly naïve and immature at time. I still had a lot to learn.

Because my financial need drove my ambition, my next internship was with a company that outsourced services. My job was to stock and record supplies. I managed what came in, and what went out.

From a list, I'd pull supplies and have it ready on a pallet for when the workers needed it. That might not seem to be a very glamorous job, but what I learned from that job was working behind a desk 9 to 5 was probably not going to work for me.

I loved the activity of that job. I rarely sat. In that job, I was always moving, interacting with people, checking and balancing. It was like I was playing sports; each time I accomplished a task, it felt like I was putting points on the board. If I didn't produce and put points on the board, it would affect the company's production. Working a job is very similar to sports. In that job I learned to be on my game all the time.

I returned to Stuart Cohen's office the next year, and this time my experience was very different. By now, I had realized I was racing a ticking clock. There was absolutely no guarantee I was going to the NFL. I really did not plan to return to my hometown to bag groceries. I was getting a first-class education, and I had the opportunity to interact with successful business people.

By now, I started noticing how people dressed in a corporate setting and I learned to copy their form of dress. If they wore business casual, I wore business casual. If they wore a tie, I wore a tie. It was time for me to assume the uniform of my team.

I had also learned the importance of networking, making and developing relationships.

When I wasn't too busy on a task, I observed the environment I worked in. How are phones answered in an office? What does a business email look like? Why would you send an email instead of a text? I saw the importance of having a schedule and gained a better understanding of the time and energy it took to run a company. Even though Mr. Cohen didn't participate in all aspects of his business, he knew what was going on and I observed his managerial skills. He was very organized. The lessons I learned in Mr. Cohen's office were extremely important for me to learn. I'm thankful he allowed me to get work experience at such a young age.

Being an athlete, I obviously love sports. A number of people outside of sports would tell me I was articulate and perhaps I should consider a career in sports commentating. Well, an internship was the perfect place to figure that out.

One summer I interned at a local radio and television station where I was responsible for editing and cutting the B-rolls. I learned the difference between voice-over and sound bites. One of my favorite experiences was learning to read off the teleprompter. There were days I would stay after work for fifteen or twenty minutes practicing in front of a camera, getting used to the speed of the teleprompter.

At this job, I realized I could learn anything, I'm coachable, and I'm very observant.

All this comes from my experience as an athlete. Because I had internships and a growing network, I found out it didn't make a huge difference what my degree was in. My degree didn't dictate what I did after school as much as my relationships and job experience did. You degree is a starting place. The thing about getting your degree is you prove to the people you are committed to finishing what you start.

My degree was in sociology, and through Campus Resources and the alumni network base at USC, I was able to land my fifth internship with a financial institute. I worked for two months there and saw them handle retirement funds worth tens of billions of dollars for major corporations. During my summer internship, I was paired up with another intern who was getting his degree in finance. At first I felt intimidated by that. By using all my transferrable skills, showing my ability to learn and adapt, the company offered me a job at the end of my internship. Not the finance major. I knew how to assume the uniform of slacks and a dress shirt. I knew how to answer the phone and be attentive when people talked to me.

All of this was happening the summer before my final season At this point, I had about a ten percent chance of going to the NFL. Rather than getting panicked about my slim chances of playing pro, I felt excited because I had choices for my future. I had a network of people I could reach out to and knew I would have a job next year, whether that meant football in the NFL or working in corporate America. I wasn't driven by fear of not being able to play football. I was excited to know, either way, once I graduated, I was going to have a job.

The Elephant in the Room

Too many times, we as student athletes want to ignore the elephant in the room, that pesky question, "What are you going to do if you don't go pro?"

In college, I ignored the question, but you don't have to follow in the footsteps of others. You can explore your answers now, rather than wait for your career to come to an end. Embrace the question! Rather than limit yourself to being just an athlete, use your time wisely and intern while being an athlete and so much more. We are all student athletes, but what else do you like to do? The athletic bubble we spend a great deal of time in is not the entire world. There is a bigger world that surrounds us, that can teach us even more. You owe it to yourself to explore the world and find your place in it. All of this can be done in addition to being a student athlete. If I went on to the NFL, great! That had been my plan from the time I was a kid.

But when I was a kid, I didn't know all the other opportunities there are in the world. My college experience is what opened my eyes to different options and opportunities. Knowing I had choices, other opportunities, took away any fear I may have had when thinking about my path following graduation.

My last summer at USC I was the busiest I had ever been. I joined my team for the 6 am workouts four days a week. Two days a week I had summer school. I took the hardest writing class, the one everyone puts off until their senior year. And I had my internship three days a week. At first I was afraid, thinking I didn't have time. I used to have that kind of limiting thinking, "I don't have time for that. I have to prepare for the biggest season of my life. I have to give it everything I've got, put all my focus into this one season if I want to go pro."

It actually became the most productive off-season I had ever had. And the most productive football season. I learned how to do it all. I became very efficient. My time management had to be on point. Everything had to be done well. I focused on doing well in workouts, so I could perform well during the next season. I had to pass the writing class, which paid me my summer stipend. I had to do the internship for the income and I didn't know if I was going on to the NFL, so I wanted to make sure this company would offer me a job if I needed one after my senior season.

When someone tells me they don't have time for an internship, it's hard for me to take them seriously.

In my mind I'm thinking, Yes you do!

I'm not the smartest person in the world. I didn't have more hours in my day than anyone else. At the time we were the number one team in the country, I was competing in my last season and the demands and expectations were extremely high.

I was still able to accomplish all these things because I managed my time, I was organized, I prioritized, and I was extremely focused.

That right there is what made my last season such a success for me. I left no stones unturned. I include these examples because all of you are capable of accomplishing everything you want athletically, academically, and professionally.

The biggest positive to having internships, you can get paid from the company and the school will pay you a stipend for taking summer school. Don't wait until you're done with your sport to find out what you are interested in. Find out while you're still on the clock. You might not have it figured out 100% but at least you will have an idea of what you do not want to do, and that is a start. As an athlete, every company wishes their current and future employees had your intangible skillset. However, they don't, which makes you a commodity. You might be behind your competitors in the sense of experience. You most likely trump them in work ethic, motivation, and teamwork. All you need is a little practice before you get in the game.

In my opinion, you don't have time to **not** do an internship.

75% of students with internships have secured a job after college.

Only 25% who do not have internships experience have a secure job after college.

Questions:

In the same way a coach won't put you in the game, an employer will not hire you if you do not have work experience.

List 3 careers are you interested in, after your playing career:

1.

_____

_____

2.

_____

_____

3.

_____

_____

If you do not know what you are interested in, list two jobs are you for sure not interested in:

1.

_____

_____

2.

_____

_____

What don't you like about these jobs?

_____

_____

_____

Salary: How much money do you want to make in your desired profession?

$_____.00

What jobs pay this amount?

_____

_____

Internships are good because:

- *They pay.*
- *They give you career options.*
- *They provide real work experience.*
- *They allow you to find out what you like and what you do not like.*

CHAPTER 19

Resume

No matter how long you play sports, there is a NEXT phase of your life. You will undoubtedly retire from playing sports at some point. It may be next week, next year, or in ten years. Very few athletes have a twenty-year professional career. Even if an athlete plays twenty years, one day they will retire and move on to the next phase of their lives.

While you're a student athlete, you get internships to get real work experience. You're doing this alongside the regular students who go to school and have no other obligations. Outside the athletic world, those same students will be your competition.

You might get an interview because of your status as a student athlete, and once you're in, you must show your worth and value. This is where a resume comes in.

It shows your value on paper. Employers automatically prefer to hire people who look qualified on paper. Every single internship you get goes on your resume. Every volunteer "job" you do should go on your resume.

You might get an interview because of your status as a student athlete, but you will be on a level playing ground once you sit down for that interview. By having a resume, both student athletes and regular students have an equal advantage. You have to play the game the same way everyone else does, and you have to follow the same rules.

Everyone who applies for an internship or a job needs a resume. In NASCAR, starting at the number one spot at the beginning gives you an advantage. The thing is, nobody cares if you started first. They care how you finish.

It's never too soon to create a resume and continue to update it as you gain different experiences. When the time comes to get a job, you'll be prepared.

Why a Resume?

Most student athletes make it into college on scholarship based on their highlight tape. This video shows all the highlights of your athletic career up to that point. By watching you in action, coaches can determine if you're talented enough and coachable enough to play for their school.

In a sense, that tape was your resume and it got you into your current position as a student athlete.

Without a tape, your chances of getting a scholarship are severely diminished.

That's exactly the same role a resume plays when you go for an interview. If you have a resume, you advance to the next level, hopefully an interview. Without a resume, it is nearly impossible to get called in for an interview. If you don't have a resume, how does a company know if you're capable of doing the job?

Not having a resume severely limits the number of opportunities you have.

As you've learned throughout this book, you have the transferrable skills employers are looking for, however, if you don't have a resume to prove it, you have no way of showing them you're self-motivated, a team player, you communicate well, work well with deadlines, and are an incredible problem solver. The only way to show them is by proving it on a resume based on your real-world experiences.

If you haven't read the chapter on Internships yet, you might want to go read that first and then come back to this chapter.

Volunteer Work

In addition to internships, many volunteer opportunities can also be used on your resume. Many student athletes learn they really enjoy a certain type of job opportunity based on a volunteer experience. It could be at a hospital, it could be as I did with the JEP program with the elementary and grade school students of LA. Every single thing you do outside school and sports shows how versatile you are. Many students forget to include their time as a volunteer on their resume.

Did you know you can add these experiences to your resume?

No Job Promised

You might be the person who has all the qualifications, but because you don't have a resume, you'll be watching much of the next part of the game from the bench. An experience I observed first-hand never allowed me to forget this lesson.

One day, during my sophomore year I saw a former teammate whose career was over after one season in the NFL.

Some of my teammates and I were hanging out at the football facility and one of them asked him, "Where are you going?" They razzed him a little because he was dressed in a suit and tie rather than workout clothes.

"I have a meeting with campus resources. They're going to get me a job."

My first thought was wow, they'll even get us a job when we're done playing. I'm in the right place.

A short twenty minutes later, the same guy who had entered the building excited and optimistic, now slammed out of the building and we could tell things hadn't gone well for him.

It turns out USC wasn't going to hand out jobs like they were Halloween candy.

It was up to us to find a job.

It was up to us to get work experience during our time as student athletes for the university in order to get a job when our athletic careers were over. That day I found out the university did not owe us anything. They paid for our services with a scholarship.

If I wanted a job when I finished going to USC and playing football, then I better have some work experience while I was a student athlete.

While my story went on to include playing five years in the NFL, there was absolutely no guarantee that was going to happen for me.

No one was in charge of my life but me.

No way was I going to mess that up.

Put that together with internships, job experiences, and you come out light years ahead of other athletes. You have to show those employers you have skills that can be transferred into any setting.

Once you know your transferrable skills, embrace them because that is what sets you apart from other applicants. You don't want to be the person with all of the qualifications but because you do not have a resume, you end up missing out on what could have been a great opportunity. It's very similar to getting a physical. You cannot play a sport without it. Even though you might have the skills to play, you might even be better than the other players on the team. Since you do not have a physical, you cannot play.

The same goes for the corporate world. Employers know you have the skills to succeed. They need it on paper to validate their intuition. Give people and employers every possible reason to hire you.

You are the type of employee every company wishes they had. But if it is not on paper and you don't have any work experience to go along with it, then it comes across as though you cannot benefit those companies. You don't have to work at internships for years, but you must have something on paper that says you have some type of work experience. A resume is something that makes companies and employers feel comfortable. It is like trying to get recruited and you don't have a bench press max or a squat max, or better yet, never ran a 40-yard dash. When you have these tests on paper, then college coaches are able to compare you to the other players in the country.

Same thing for the business world. When they see something that you have done on paper, it makes them feel better about you as a potential candidate.

It's All About Choices

When I finished playing and I was no longer an athlete, I wanted to have choices. I wanted the opportunity to choose what career I wanted to go into. Whenever I got placed in a box or there was a glass ceiling over my head, I got agitated. In order to have choice and prevent society from placing me in a box, I knew I had to diversify myself through various work experiences each off-season.

It gave me more exposure, more access to different experiences. I never wanted to stick with only one internship.

While I went to Stuart Cohen for two internships, the only reason I returned because I knew I didn't learn all the lessons I could the first time around. And that second time, I really maximized my time there.

Diversify yourself during your college years because you have the opportunities. While you're in school, you can do several internships to find out what you like and what you don't like to do.

Finding out what you don't want to do is just as important as discovering what you like to do.

If you recall, when I wanted to get more playing time Ken Norton, Jr. coached me well when he gave me the advice to become versatile. I saw myself as just a "middle linebacker" but he recommended I play all three linebacker positions. He told me the more I do the more I would get. That meant playing time on the team and more opportunity to be seen by NFL scouts.

My lightbulb went off right then. At that moment, I was given information that would get me drafted and allowed for me to play in the NFL. It was also life-changing information I applied and still apply today in my everyday living.

Making Up Time

If you don't take advantage of the internship opportunities during your off season, you may eventually have to get jobs you do not wish to have, simply to get work experience.

My advice to you is this: become versatile. Be more, do more, so you have the skills that give you more opportunities in life.

Yes, for me, playing multiple linebacker positions was not fun. I hated every minute of learning new positions. I felt like a jack-of-all-trades and a master of none, but being a jack-of-all-trades is what got me drafted by the Jacksonville Jaguars.

Because of my versatility, I was able to be interchangeable. At any given moment, I could play three or four different positions. The value of that for the teams in the NFL was they could pay one salary while they were getting multiple players.

Same thing with a resume.

As an athlete, you can do so many things.

One day you may meet with an employer who may say to you, "You can do many things, great. We have several jobs you have the skill sets for, but they're already filled. However, we have one here and I see you have the exact skill set we need. Welcome aboard."

Being versatile opens the door.

Getting in the door is all you need.

Once you get in the door with professional attire, you look like you belong, act like you belong, and you have the opportunity to succeed in the same way as you did as an athlete.

I'm where I am today because USC took a chance on me and I took advantage of every opportunity I saw. I filled out my resume in order to look like a valuable person to any prospective employer. So far, I'm running my own business and I'm still adding to my resume. You never know when someone will ask you for a resume, It's better to have a resume and not need it, than to need one and not have it.

It's all about having choices and opportunities.

You might not see it right now but, you will appreciate having options when your career is over.

Questions:

Do you have a current resume? If not, your first responsibility is to create one.

What resources are at your disposal to get assistance with your resume?

Highlights to include on a resume:

Personal Information

- Name
- Phone number
- Address
- Email address

Education

- University
- Years attended
- Degree focus
- Outstanding recognition

Work experience

- Part time jobs
- Internships
- Volunteer work
- Awards

Athletics

- Sports played
- Years played

- Accolades/Awards
- Skills you have gained from participating in collegiate sports

Other

- Memberships to organizations
- Military experiences
- Computer skills
- Awards
- Hobbies

As a student athlete, your resume shows:

- *You're accountable for yourself and your goals.*
- *You are used to working in a team environment.*
- *You can balance academics and sports.*
- *You're used to accomplishing tasks.*

CHAPTER 20

Exit Strategy

Once you embrace the fact sports will end and there is life after your playing career, you understand it is never too early to start preparing for your exit.

~Thomas R. Williams

If you read the networking chapter where Keith Rivers shared his thoughts on looking at the various stages of your sports career as closing one business and opening another, you're well on your way to understanding your exit plan.

This is *not* where I'm telling you to give up your plans to become a professional athlete. I want every athlete to experience sports after college. Play as long as you can. Leave no doubt you gave it everything you had. Because some of you are going to play professional sports.

But the truth of the matter is fewer than 1% of all collegiate athletes go on to play sports professionally. That means some of you reading this book are facing the closing of this business of playing collegiate sports and moving on to your next business.

That right there is exciting news.

Congratulations!

Those of you who do go on to play professionally, again, congratulations. You cannot become complacent. Your career is only as stable as your body and your fate is in the eyes and hands of professional teams who want to pay you to play for them. I've watched plenty of teammates and opponents go from a really promising career to being permanently sidelined in the blink of an eye from an injury.

You never plan on being injured.

I didn't.

While I tried really hard to make a solid comeback, my reality hit me when I realized I either needed to walk away from the game, or I might never walk again.

It was not the way I'd imagined my career ending. I wasn't quite as prepared as I might have liked. In fact, I wish I had this book in my hands at that moment when I had to leave my hotel room and take the long walk to another part of the hotel until the team could arrange my transportation back to LA.

The end of my NFL career didn't come with trumpets and a giant celebration. I didn't have a press conference or a party. It was more like a hurried escort out of the building.

On my flight from the East Coast to the West Coast, I took out a notebook and started writing. I wrote about my dreams, my plans, my hopes, and my fears. My NFL career had ended. As with many of us, it ended a lot sooner than I expected.

I was now forced to answer that question, the one I purposefully hid from.

What's NEXT?

Immediately after my career in the NFL, I had plenty of people who gave my what they considered to be solid advice, "Thomas, it's time to join the real world now. Time to get a real job."

But what exactly did that mean?

To me, playing sports at both the collegiate and the professional level *was* a job! I got up early, I practiced for hours and hours a day. I stayed late if I didn't understand a play. You can't tell me that didn't take effort, drive, and dedication. Why were people telling me I had been living in a fantasy land?

The truth hit me.

Those who were giving me advice had lingering regrets about the fact they never got a chance to play ball at the level I had played. They had a mortgage, car payments, kids and a spouse to take care of. Most of them had jobs they didn't even like.

Why would I take advice from them?

The real truth about developing an exit plan is that it is all up to you.

Every single chapter in this book was written for you. I designed it for you to answer the questions we have at various points in our careers. Fortunately for me, opportunities presented themselves to me in college and I was able to take advantage of them. I networked with people. I developed relationships. I did a number of internships where I learned what I liked to do and what I didn't like to do once my career was over.

So on that airplane trip home, I listed everything I loved about playing football. My favorite was I worked really, really hard for six months out of the year and then I could do what I wanted to do for the other six months out of the year. What kind of a job could I do that would give me that kind of flexibility?

Little by little, I asked myself the very questions you find at the end of every chapter in this book. What did I want to do? I already had a pretty good idea of what I did *not* want to do. I realized I loved talking to people, sharing my knowledge, things I'd learned. At this very moment, I identified my PASSION. It occurred to me I wanted to work with people. I had experienced a DREAM turned reality and I wanted to help people realize and live their dreams.

Look around you. There are many people in transition today. With the economic downturn, thousands of people have had to re-invent themselves, find ways to utilize their skills in a new way. Just as a college athlete needs to do.

That chapter on transferrable skills? That's one of the most important chapters in this book. In fact, go back and read it again. Don't take anyone's word for it that because you played sports, you're washed up once your sports career is over. That couldn't be further from the truth.

I once heard someone say you should never take advice from someone who has never been in your shoes. Why would you take advice from someone who has never played sports at the elite collegiate level you've played? They have no idea what they're talking about.

This is the focus of my book.

I've been there. I attained the pinnacle of an athletic career and then moved on to professional sports. I loved my years in the NFL, but they ended more abruptly than I wanted. I was not washed up. Not by a long shot. I took an inventory of my transferrable skills and discovered because of my athletic background, I was more qualified for just about any job I wanted. As athletes, we all are!

In terms of transferrable skills, you're an expert already. Everything sports has taught us is transferrable to the next phase of your life. You transitioned from high school to college athletics. Academically, you took the study habits you learned in high school and transferred them to college. Yes, you learned some new habits and skills in college, but I wanted you to understand you TRANSITIONED.

The secret about gaining new skills is you now have more tools in your tool belt, and you never have to give them back. They're yours. You earned them. Certain plays in college were called one thing, in the NFL they call the same play something different. You might watch film in college, and that same task in the corporate world is called data analysis or market research. No matter what it is called, you have been doing it for years. It might have a different name.

It's a Breakup – And It Will Sting

Don't get me wrong, leaving the NFL prematurely hurt. I was sad. In shock. Wondered what I would do the next day because for so many years I did exactly what I was either told or expected to do. The biggest shock, I think, was I was suddenly the only one in charge of my life.

As athletes, we were never in complete control of our lives. We have never been coached to be in complete control.

Leaving the NFL was a breakup.

I don't know any other way to put it. It was unexpected. I had to allow myself the opportunity to recognize that, see it for what it was, and grieve that loss. What I was *not* going to do was to look at my college years at USC or my years in the NFL and live in the past for the rest of my life.

It was not who I was.

It was only what I did.

I was not football. Football was just a part of me.

If anyone were to ask me what was the best thing I did for myself following my football career, I would tell them, for me, it was when I went to get counseling.

I did and with what I have learned I could fill a dozen books. The most critical aspect of counseling was I was able to get a different perspective on my life as an athlete, and figure out what parts of me were a football player and which parts of me were Thomas. Some of the behaviors that served me well as a football player might not be the very best behaviors for me outside of football.

Face it, when you become an athlete at this level, it takes a lot of drive, dedication, determination, and just a little bit of insanity thrown in there.

What we did was not normal.

To get up at 5 am and run wind sprints before the sun comes up tends to make us erratic. Not while you're participating in your sport, because you need that to keep going. Once you have moved on to the next phase of your life, that type of thinking won't serve us.

Talking to someone who understands what we have gone through as athletes can give us a new perspective, allowing us to see promise in our future and because of that, we should be excited about what is to come.

Moving On

You may be part of the fewer than 1% who continues their athletic career after college. GREAT! The number we overlook is 100% of athletes who play sports have to retire.

Many times in our careers, we hear the words backup plan or, "What if you don't make it?"

I never want an athlete to have a backup plan. Do not take your eyes off the ultimate goal. I've learned you can't go very far with a backup plan. What I wish for every single student athlete is to have additional plans. Plans you have while you are working on the ultimate goal. In addition to playing sports, what else are you capable of doing?

You are much *more* than an athlete.

Say it as many times as you need to in order to believe it.

Once you believe it, it's time to take action. It's time to start to believe you truly are more than an athlete.

What do you want to do when your career comes to an end? When you are no longer an athlete, what do you want to be remembered for outside of sports? What will your legacy be?

The more time you spend thinking about these questions now, the less uncertain you will be when the day comes. Preparation makes us confident athletes. Preparation does not stop with sports. It applies to all areas of our lives.

When you have an exit strategy, your transition will be a big step forward to something you expect rather than a giant leap over a canyon you're not sure you can cross.

In sports we always had the next play, next game, or the next season to look forward and prepare for.

When it comes to life, we have no clue, and that is scary. You don't want to get to the end of your career and have nothing to look forward to. Find your passion, create a vision and attack it, the same way you did your sport.

The game uses us. Our bodies, our minds, and takes our time.

Once it is done, it's over.

But remember this, the game also prepares us. You don't have to reinvent the wheel when you transition. You have already invented the wheel. How will you decide to use your passions and your transferrable skills?

You must see yourself doing something outside of sports.

You *are* more than an athlete.

Questions:

I want you to take a moment and write down your exit from sports. Let's say you are 35 years-old and have graduated college with a degree. You have just finished your professional career of ten years.

In your opinion, did you accomplish everything you wanted to in your athletic career?

_____

_____

What do you want to do next?

_____

_____

_____

_____

Who would be the first person you would reach out to, to get guidance on transitioning from being an athlete to life after sports?

_____

_____

_____

Did you complete your degree?

_____

Write down three skills have you mastered as an athlete that will transfer into your next career?

1.

_____

2.

_____

3.

_____

Name two work experiences that you have had that you can place on a resume:

1.

_____

2.

_____

Who are the two most influential people you have developed a relationship with who are in your network?

1.

_____

_____

2.

_____

_____

What do you want your life's legacy to be, moving forward?

_____

_____

_____

Even though your career is not over, even though you are a student athlete, do you feel confident enough to answer these questions? If not, what else do you need?

_____

_____

_____

I'm not saying to constantly be looking forward to the day when your career ends, all I'm saying is the more answers you have to these questions, the easier your transition will be.

CHAPTER 21

Still Playing the Game

I once attended a presentation called "After the Cheering Stops," designed to prepare me for life after my football career. I was in my second year at USC and I couldn't pay attention to the presentation, because I kept saying to myself, the cheering will *never* stop.

Not for me.

And most student athletes I've spoken with across the country feel the same way.

On one hand that's wonderful, because it means you're filled with fire, passion, and confidence. On the other hand, the reality is, none of us can play sports forever.

One morning, I spoke with my old coach, Ken Norton, Jr. and he reminded me while I may no longer be a football player, I never stop playing the game. He said, "Discover new ways to stay motivated. Once we can identify our passion, that is when we have another reason to get out of the bed with excitement each and every single morning."

Ken asked me, "What did football mean to you?"

What a great question that was. I realized, as I looked back over my many, many years of playing football I had learned some spectacular skills. I began to count them off on my fingers in terms of transferrable skills: leadership, goal oriented, ability to strategize, and the list went on and on. I came to the conclusion that football, for me, was my foundation. It was the foundation for what has made me into the man I am today. And I bet for you, your participation in sports has been the same. It is your foundation for who you are today.

My realization, then, was the game never, ever stops. There might not be fans in the stands or a jersey on my back, but the game has always been life. I still strategize, I still network, I still make a schedule for what things need to get done and what things I need to practice, I'm still preparing for my next game whether it's my next speaking engagement, a meeting with my editor or my marketing team, it's an endless "to do" list. When we, as athletes, retire, we often become mediocre. It doesn't have to be that way. Complacency is our opponent each and every single day. There is always something new to learn, and as Coach Carroll instilled in all of his players, competing every single day, always looking for an edge to get better has become a daily challenge.

I am who I am today because of who I was as an athlete. I never intend to throw away that blueprint.

When faced with doubts or questions about whether I'm able to tackle my next challenge, I remember what I was able to accomplish in sports. I encourage you to do the same. Don't go back to live, just look back. It is there to remind you how much drive and passion you have.

Try it for yourself. When you think you haven't accomplished anything; look back.

When you think you don't have enough endurance to keep going; look back.

When you don't think you can achieve the impossible; look back. When you think you're average, look back. You have done more in a short period of time than most will ever do in a lifetime.

There are times I find myself in a room with a number of high-powered business professionals. Initially I was intimidated and insecure. A moment shifted my thinking when a man told me how he had always wanted to play sports on the biggest stage. He said, "I've always wanted to do what you have been able to accomplish." The man was in his sixties, and while he might have been worth millions of dollars, not a single dollar could buy him the experience I had earned myself.

Instantly I gained the confidence I thought I lacked. As athletes, all of us know what it takes to get something done. We've done it and we can do it over and over again. You know what passion feels like. You know what long days and short nights will accomplish. You're very familiar with the reward that comes from those kind of sacrifices. Perseverance, obstacles? As athletes, we have all mastered those. Every single one of you who play collegiate sports has what it takes to successfully transition. Now your job is to identify those transferrable skills. Build those relationships. Understand the dynamic and leverage the status of being a student athlete. Use all those skills you've learned and you will continue to live a life full of GREATNESS!

You have everything you need to get everything you want.

Climbing to the top of the mountain wasn't always easy, was it? As you slowly progressed upward, people fell off the track. Maybe it wasn't in their cards, but for all of us it was. As you move forward you may need to separate yourself from the athlete, but never forget the athlete you were.

Another piece of advice I received from a successful athlete-turned businessman is this: "Stay in the building long enough." I didn't understand at first what he meant. He reminded me most NFL general managers got to where they are today because they stayed in the building long enough. They started out as ball boys. Then they moved up to being a scout. Then they were directors of college scouting. Then directors of pro scouting. They stayed in the building long enough.

When he put it in terms like that, I completely understood. That is the advice I'm sharing with you. Just get in the door. Stay in the building long enough.

If we stay around long enough, we'll observe enough, learn enough, move up enough to finally reach that place we want to be.

It's no different than when I was on that last flight home from the NFL. I decided I wanted to become a public speaker. How did I prepare? I talked. I talked to every single person I came in contact with. I talked to people at the gas station, the bus stop, even the person on the corner waiting to cross the street. I knew by "staying in the building" long enough I would get better over time and soon I would find people who would pay me to speak.

It's no different than knocking on that door, going to see the coach on your day off, showing up when it wasn't mandatory. Keep showing up. Because eventually coach is going to need a player and if you're the one always showing up, he's going to pick you.

My dream was to be a football player. My end goal was the NFL. I didn't care how I got there. To get there, I became versatile. I wasn't just a middle linebacker. I was a linebacker and I could play any linebacker position. That made me valuable.

Very often, we become attached to a specific path that will lead us to our ultimate goals. The truth is, many times life has a different path for us that may lead us to the desired outcome or goal that we have in mind, or not. Most of the time, we get discouraged when the path to the place we want to go is different than what we expect. Focusing on the end goal is extremely important, but sometimes we will get there by a completely different path than the one we have envisioned. Be invested in the dream and flexible in the way you get that dream. Go with all your effort! Successful people don't dip their toe in the water, they jump all the way in.

Stay in the building long enough. Keep playing until you master the necessary skills. Go back to being a rookie again or your freshman year. Remember how hard you had to work to overcome that learning curve? It's no different. Same skills, different game.

Stay in the building.

Keep showing up.

That's what football was to me. Hang around the people who already know what you want to learn. Life is a bigger picture than just sports. Participating in sports is nothing more than a single play in the big picture of life.

Ask yourself this, when you were a kid and said you wanted to play sports, whether you were eight or eighteen, where did you see yourself going to college? Wherever you ended up going doesn't matter. The only thing that matters is you ended up at a university getting an education and playing college sports.

Your next question will be this: Where do you see yourself when your career is over? Who have you become? What is your legacy? What will you be known for after your athletic career? What do you want to put all your effort and passion into just as you have with sports?

How great do you want to be?

Someone once told me once my career was over I had to get real and leave fantasyland. I disagree. I liked living in fantasyland where I believed everything I wanted to do was possible. Do you believe that? Will you believe the person who says you have to come back to reality and live a normal mundane life?

I'm not here to tell you how to live. I'm only sharing that I played pro ball for five years and it seems like a lifetime ago when I left the NFL. It's not because I left fantasyland. It's because I opened myself up to every opportunity I believed in and I'm doing something more impactful and greater than even my NFL career.

The day I left the NFL I called my dad and was so nervous about telling him my career was over. I thought he would be disappointed in me. He said, "Son, your words will be more impactful than any hit you ever had on the football field."

My dad was right. I'm still playing the game, I just don't tackle people any more.

For me, the game has never ended.

Ask yourself, will you be relentless in pursuing your greatness for the rest of your life?

ABOUT THOMAS R. WILLIAMS

Thomas R. Williams, owner of Thomas R. Williams, Inc., is an author and professional speaker. After graduating from USC where he won two National Championships, Thomas was selected in the 2008 NFL Draft. After a five-year NFL career, Thomas now dedicates his time and efforts teaching student athletes how they can maximize their time and status while playing collegiate sports. Using information from national entrepreneurial conferences and corporate boardrooms, Thomas works around the country to transcend the thinking of today's student athlete.

GREATNESS does not stop when the scoreboard turns off. It is a life style.

In 2016, Thomas started his 501c3, PURSUITS of Greatness; an organization that gives tailored suits to former student athletes who have exhausted all of their athletic eligibility. The suit represents a new uniform for each former student athlete as they transition to the next phase of their lives.

Made in the USA
San Bernardino, CA
12 August 2016